ABIDING CHRISTIAN VOL 2

UNCONDITIONALLY CHRIST'S

IIIIIIIIIIIIIIIIIIIIIIIIIIIII
I0149403

Martha Olawale

Copyright - After God Heart Inc.

550 Congressional Blvd. STE 350, Carmel IN, 46032

Follow on Facebook - https://www.facebook.com/AbidingChristians

Follow on Twitter - https://x.com/AbidinChristian

Websites: aftergodheart.org and abidingchristian.com

FOREWORD

In a time when "as Christians, it's easy to fall into a routine in our walk with God. We go to Church, read the Bible, pray for our daily bread," Martha invites us to go deeper. The "Abiding Christian" is Martha asking us to journey with her as she's "returning to the simplicity of opening my Bible and allowing the Holy Spirit to guide me through its depth and richness."

Within these pages and woven around personal stories, you would see clearly Martha's love for the Lord, how deeply she cherishes the Bible and how personal she applies the precious words that flow from it. She challenges everyone with a timeless truth that the Bible is "not just a collection of stories; it's a book of godly principles and promises to help us navigate an incredibly complex world."

I find this book to be practical and very relatable. And having known Martha since we were teenagers from our first year of College, it's a joy to read the love and depth of the Word flowing from her to bless the Body of Christ.

When Jesus visited Martha and Mary, the Bible says, "Mary sat down attentively before the Master, absorbing every revelation he shared." Luke 10:38-39 TPT

It's my prayer that as you travel through the pages of this book, you will come to love sitting with the Word and experiencing all the glorious transformations that await you.

Lanre Onasanya
Pastor
Spirit of Life Christian Centre
Ontario, Canada.

TABLE OF CONTENTS

PREFACE

I can still see myself pulling the cover over my face as Mum rings the bell for prayers around 6 am each morning. I never got used to that or the 9 pm daily family prayers. I didn't want to sing hymns in the morning or when I could still watch the television before going to bed, but she made us do it. A simple "Our Father, who hath in Heaven" would have been okay for me, but Mum had a mini-Church service in our home twice daily.

To my mother, starting the day and ending it with Jesus was the only way she was assured her children would grow up strong enough to face the world. She loved God, and it won't take more than a few minutes to know who she lives for when you meet her. I am a product of what I would call "Rebecca Aderibigbe's School of Ministry." Although she's not here, I live my life conscious of how much she loved Jesus despite the constraints around her. I was the fifth child of a family of seven, and I genuinely believe that my life and how I relate with and honor God thrives on my memory of her life with God.

The Abiding Christian volumes are compilations of articles first published on the abidingchristian.com website weekly and edited for book publishing. They are short reflections on applicable life lessons rooted in the principle that God, in His divine power, has indeed given us all things that pertain to life and godliness (2 Peter 1:3). *The articles are non-sequential; they are independent of one another and written at different times with different emotions but inspired by one God.* As you read, as I am learning at the foot of the cross, you'll discover that our Savior and King perfect our existence, and Jesus is enough for whatever life throws at us.

God reveals His mysteries by simplifying and interpreting the scriptures with the Holy Spirit's help; we just need to open our Bibles. When we surrender to Him, the Holy Spirit will reduce the complexity of understanding how to apply scriptural principles to our daily experiences. It doesn't mean we'll always have the answer to all questions, but we'll be assured of God's presence even through difficult seasons.

This is the second volume of the Abiding Christian books, and it was published at the same time as the first because the manuscript was too large for a single book. As you read, you will learn what it means to be unconditionally Christ's. While Heaven is the goal, our road through Earth comes with demands that tug at our hearts, and only God-consciousness can help us live in Heaven's honor.

ACKNOWLEDGMENT

Mum, thank you for showing me Jesus and the beauty of a life lived for Him and that He is worth it all. Your difficulties didn't deter your faith, and the happy times didn't restrict it. Your walk with God symbolized a love story beyond human comprehension. And, Dad, thank you for teaching me strength and courage.

Seunmi, I love you; I love your heart for God, its tenderness, kindness, humility, and strength. Thank you for holding me these past decades, daily telling me, "From your home, you will impact the world for Christ." Your leadership and support made Abiding Christian happen. You fight like a champion on your knees and lead with grace. And Desayo, Joseph, and RonDaniel, I love you; I love the sound of your TV shows, your loud praise music (minus the headache after), and your loft area laughter. God made you my heritage, my joy, and a source of peace in a very challenging world. Thank you for making this Mum thing effortless for me.

I started the Abiding Christian website during COVID-19, and while there seemed to be so much to write about at the time, it was difficult for me to write. It was a heavy season for me, as it was for everyone else. I was exhausted from the uproar and uncertainty in the world, but despite that, God's strength was made perfect in my weariness through my friends.

Thank you to everyone who has encouraged my walk with Jesus and made navigating the world easier, and to all my friends with whom I have shared life. Those who have been part of my journey for almost forty years (Dr. Mariam Oluyemi), to friends I walk with today. I am grateful for the Thieneman Circle and the joy of walking with them as we grow in our identity (Shannon, extra point). Proverbs 11:25 says, *"The liberal soul shall prosper, and he that watereth shall be watered also himself."*

To all Abiding Christian readers, thank you for reading and heeding the call for us to go deeper in our pursuit of godliness. It pays to walk with Jesus! You are the reason God gave me this charge, and I am grateful for you.

To my Savior, my King, my fortress, and Shepherd, my helper, the Lord Jesus, thank you, Sir, for loving me unconditionally and for all your sacrifices. Thank you for sending the Holy Spirit and stilling the storms in my soul so I could see God beyond the clouds. *"Now unto the King eternal, immortal, invisible, the only wise God, be honor and glory forever and ever. Amen."* 1 Timothy 1:17.

PART I

HE THAT WALKS WITH THE WISE

"Walk with the wise and become wise."
Proverbs 13:20a

There is no such thing as common sense in our world anymore. Simple innate reasonings are now clouded and convoluted with human erroneous suppositions. To be wise, we must look through the lens with which God sees things and listen with ears tuned to the frequency of Heaven. **Proverbs 2:6** says, *"For the Lord gives wisdom, and from his mouth come knowledge and understanding."* It is anything but wise if it is not from God or aligns with His precepts.

I began my Christian journey as a teenager, and over the years, I have witnessed God increase me in every area of my life. I could not have survived the battles and mazes of my path without Christ. As I study His Word, my vision becomes clearer, and as I listen to His voice, the clogs in my ears dissolve. He guides with grace and precision, lovingly leading His children through each season of life.

Though we are born with God's nature, our brokenness creates a struggle in defining right from wrong. Yet, no matter how dark the valley may seem, God always finds a way to teach us through His Holy Spirit, surrounding us with the right people in each season. He directs us to the right messages at the right times and blesses us with friends who pour wisdom into our hearts through their love for God. I have been privileged to meet some of these people along my journey; they are the treasures of my life. From my years in Nigeria to nearly two decades away from it, God has placed me in the right circles to preserve His call over my life.

None of us has life completely figured out; we all need people to hold our hands when we grow weary and remind us of what truly matters. I am neither an island nor self-sustained; I am active in the Kingdom's work because I walk with the wise. I am surrounded by friends whose hearts beat toward Heaven and who long to honor God. They are a unique breed—warriors and fruit-bearers in a desert land. Together, we are strategically positioned to inspire one another to keep saying "yes" to God and to put on our battle armor. In this pivotal season of my life, an hour with the Thieneman Circle is worth much more. When we gather, something powerful happens. It is as if we are in a command center, strengthening and encouraging one another.

Wisdom is both contextual and dynamic; it cannot be contained. It pours down from hearts that yearn for God. No human has all the answers, but little drops of wisdom from godly friends can turn a spark into a giant fire in your mind. Put simply, it is wise to walk with the wise—not as the world defines it, but with those surrendered to the life, death, and resurrection of Jesus. If you want to know God's heart and find rest in a restless world, walk closely with the Holy Spirit. He will lead you to honor God and surround you with people who spur you toward godliness, hold you accountable to Heaven's mandate, and speak to the warrior within you.

SAVED TO FLOURISH IN RIGHTEOUSNESS

"You heavens above, rain down my righteousness; let the clouds shower it down. Let the earth open wide, let salvation spring up, let righteousness flourish with it; I, the Lord, have created it." **Isaiah 45:8**

Saved! That is a word any captive would love to hear. A person held hostage by an enemy looks forward to the day of rescue. Every day in bondage seems longer because it is neither home nor the place the prisoner wants to be. How you breathe, think, and move in freedom is different from your experience in bondage. Everything about you changes when you are rescued from prison; even what and how you eat changes.

If you subscribe to the idea that your gift of salvation is a ticket to ride on the train of ungodliness, you might want to check the fine print. 1 John 3:9 says, *"No one who is born of God will continue to sin, because God's seed remains in them; they cannot go on sinning, because they have been born of God."* Like a seed in the ground, we might not fully bring forth our fruits of righteousness, but we should continue to grow in it. Essentially, our salvation should produce righteousness, not sin. Our messes and prison meals should become distasteful and uncomfortable, and our new identity should draw us to the Father's heart.

There must be bondage before freedom and a mess before a cleanup. You are saved from something—not to continue in that thing but to leave it behind. The day of salvation comes with unlocked chains when the prisoner stands and speaks with renewed strength.

Why roll in filth when you can sit in a crystal-clear pool? Isaiah 45:8b says, *"Let salvation spring up. Let righteousness flourish with it."* Salvation is the seed, and the fruit of salvation is righteousness. Who I was before Christ is not who I want to be again. The old me was a confused, unworthy mess; the new me is a free, beloved daughter of God. We are saved to flourish in righteousness, to crave what our Father loves, and to return to God's original intent for humanity.

THE BIBLE: THE LIVING WORD

"For the Word of God is alive and active. Sharper than any double-edged sword, it penetrates even to dividing soul and spirit, joints and marrow; it judges the thoughts and attitudes of the heart." **Hebrews 4:12**

While unpacking a box, we found a Bible I used a few decades ago. As soon as I saw it, I knew it. It was a close friend I had carried with me everywhere for years. I remember sitting on my bed reading it and in church, flipping the pages according to the preacher's directions. Seeing the compact blue Bible in my husband's hand almost brought me to tears. No other book in the world but my Bible can make me feel that way. I remember the treasures I discovered in the pages of that Bible. The inside of the covers is filled with my writing. One of those writings is an affirmation I wrote before I met my husband: *"I am the daughter of the Lord, in whom He is well pleased… it is my heritage to be gloriously married."* (2000)

In a world growing rapidly, it is easy to lose sight of the blessings in seemingly small things. It is now a world of "the more, the better." But is it truly better to have more of everything? With the advent of information and technology came the boom in demand for more. Sadly, we want more options for everything and even more additions to God's Word.

When asked about my Bible study habits, I often refer to devotionals from trusted Christian leaders like Pastors David Jeremiah and Charles Stanley. However, I always stress the joy of opening the raw, unfiltered pages of the Bible myself. In the early years of my Christian faith, learning from Bishop David Oyedepo taught me that. I seek to approach scripture with the awe of underground Christians who, if given a choice, would die for just a few pages of the Bible—unlike Western world Christians who might cower in the face of opposition despite all their books and resources. God's Word has been a guiding light, leading me to where I am today. ***Psalm 119:105*** aptly describes it as a lamp illuminating my path.

Understandably, the prospect of understanding the Bible can be overwhelming. However, we can take comfort in knowing that the Holy Spirit is our guide. As Jesus assured us in John 16:13, "*However, when He, the Spirit of Truth, is come, He will guide you into all truth; for He shall not speak from Himself, but whatsoever He shall hear, that shall He speak; and He will show you things to come.*" Trusting the Holy Spirit's guidance can give us the reassurance and direction we need in our Bible study journey.

Think of this: I was fifteen when I started reading the Bible alone. I was a high schooler, and there were many reasons to improve my English language skills, yet it impacted me. I can still feel the joy that filled my spirit when I opened my first Bible after being born again. That is almost four decades ago, and I still clearly remember what that first Bible looked like. Although we had many Bibles at home, my dad gave me that Bible, and it was mine—only mine. It was brown, with larger letters than my newly found blue friend. I could not get enough of the thrill that came with learning to live by the dictates of God's Word, and I wore that Bible out in just a few years.

I love timelines and backgrounds, but we must remember not to lose the message the Holy Spirit intends for us to grasp as we read. "It is written" is enough to touch the right chords in our souls. One word, a phrase, a verse, or a chapter—whatever it is—let it be the Holy Spirit's interpretation. We can do our research for knowledge but expect an encounter with the first Word as we read the Bible.

Quoting scripture works. Jesus often quoted the Old Testament with a simple sentence or reference like *"It is written."* For instance, speaking of His authority to testify about Himself, He referred the Pharisees to Deuteronomy 17:6, saying, *"In your own Law it is written that the testimony of two witnesses is true."* Also, in John 19:46, He simplified the complex details of temple cleansing by quoting Isaiah 56:7: *"My house will be a house of prayer, but you have made it a den of robbers."* We can't know the Bible better than Jesus; after all, He was the Word of God from the beginning *(John 1:1),* so trusting the scripture as Jesus did will do us good.

The younger, hungrier Christian in me says, *"Trust the Holy Spirit"* to reveal the truth of God's Word to you. Approach the Bible as God's guide for your life. He will tell you what you need to hear each time you read it. It is not just a collection of stories; it's a book of godly principles and promises to help us navigate an incredibly complex world. I am here because God's Word works and can bring meaning to any life.

Hebrews 4:12 says it is *'living.'* A single word in the Bible is worth more than a million words elsewhere; it is more than letters—every word in it can change your life. It changed mine because, without the truth from the pages of the Bible, I would not be where I am today, doing what I am doing with my life and impacting people's lives as God has positioned me to do.

We are filling our minds with too much "junk knowledge" to enjoy the abundant treasure of filtering our understanding through the Holy Spirit's lens. We'd rather quote cute statements from people and books than God's Word. The problem is that these quotes provide a temporary *"sugar rush"* that fades quickly. They don't last because they are letters that kill, not the Spirit that gives life *(2 Corinthians 3:6).*

While I embrace the blessing of many resources from verified sources, especially those that help me study the Bible, I can't deny the purity and simplicity of learning from the Spirit of Truth Himself. I would choose the Holy Spirit over a billion sources. It's His Word, and He knows what I need when needed. One verse has had countless meanings in my life because there is something new to learn each time I read or hear it. If my understanding were limited to a single person's interpretation or research, I would miss the many layers of the Holy Spirit's interpretation.

As my vision blurred, I got another Bible because the lettering in my blue friend was too small for me. I've had more Bibles since then, but seeing this one awakened something in me. It reminded me of how easy it was to take God at His Word, even when it seemed complicated. If a fifteen-year-old me were willing to follow Christ as I read His Word, it would produce the same resolve in anyone. Although my Bible today is much bigger, heavier, and harder to carry everywhere, I will treat it as I once treated this little friend. I am returning to the simplicity of opening my Bible and allowing the Holy Spirit to guide me through its depth and richness.

AN UNDIVIDED HEART

"Teach me your way, Lord, that I may rely on your faithfulness; give me an undivided heart, that I may fear your name." **Psalm 86:11**

How can I have an undivided heart in a world of countless daily choices? As I read this verse in the Book of Psalms, I paused and pondered it for a while. God is not joking or willing to share my heart with anything or anyone; He wants all of it.

I love my husband, my kids, my family, my church, my friends, and the people God brings my way as I journey through life, but all the love I have for them rests upon a single foundation: my passion for Christ alone. While my heart seems drawn in many directions, ensuring it draws from a single source is essential. Every emotion I feel—anger, pain, loss, joy, peace—should find wholeness in God.

With this realization, it is essential that we examine our lives closely to see where we have allowed things other than

God to take precedence. Have I divided my heart into smaller pieces, justifying giving God the most considerable portion as a big deal as if it were mine to give? God is not asking us to make Him the best of all; He is asking us to make Him our all in all.

An undivided heart is rooted in the fullness of God's love and trust in Him. It is a heart that longs for its Maker with hope, knowing He is always there. It's a heart that yearns for God to be magnified in every area of life. It relies completely on its Creator for sustenance. It is poor and needy, always seeking God's help. As David said in the opening verses of **Psalm 86,** *"Hear me, Lord, and answer me, for I am poor and needy. Guard my life, for I am faithful to you."*

The beauty and worth of our lives lie in our willingness to give them back to God, beginning with our hearts. **Proverbs 23:26 says,** *"My son, give me your heart, and let your eyes find happiness in my ways."* All our ways must align with His way. God is not saying to sit in a room and chant His name repeatedly; rather, He invites us to honor Him as we go about our days—laughing, eating, talking, learning, teaching, and living the life He has blessed us with—remembering that everything is encompassed in His love for us.

COME BOLDLY, NOT CARELESSLY

"Speak unto all the congregation of the children of Israel and say unto them: 'Ye shall be holy, for I the Lord your God am holy," **Leviticus 19:2.**

God has been dealing with me on holiness for a while. Although I've been a Christian since I was a teen and made God's grace my blanket for decades, the stirring in my soul leaves me asking, *"Does grace erase my need for holiness?"* Also, *"Did Christ's death reduce God's love for righteousness?"*

As I read through the Old Testament, I see God's desire for how He wants His people to live. He tried rules, commandments, judges, and kings to get them to live right, but the haughtiness of the human spirit wrestles with that. God couldn't be more explicit than He was when He told Moses in Leviticus 19:2, "Speak unto all the congregation of the children of Israel and say unto them: 'Ye shall be holy, for I the Lord your God am holy."

The idea that grace somehow reduces God's holiness is false; it's dangerous, and many Christians have bought into it. We hide behind grace instead of living by grace. God is still God and an equal part of the Trinity, and Christ's life, death, and ascension did not dethrone Him or erase His call to His people to live holy. Grace should strengthen my resolve to come boldly to the throne to obtain mercy and help in times of need *(Hebrews 4:16)*. Grace is not for me to wallow in my dirt but for me to receive strength to live free from my dirt, so I can be the picture God saw when He created humanity.

Change is not part of God's nature, and our salvation ticket does not cloud the beauty of His glory. He said in Malachi 3:6, "For I am the Lord, I change not." He can't change who He is, but our redemption leads us through transformation. We need to change; God does not; He loves clean, and if we love God, we will desire to live as He loves to see us live.

God is righteous and orderly. When we relegate His call to pursue holiness to the abyss of our minds, we embrace a primitive nature that should be buried at the foot of the cross. Christ's death carries the power for us to live holy, not carelessly. Grace is a gift that empowers us to live up to God's expectations, not lower His expectations of humanity.

Peter's words in *1 Peter 1:15*, under the new covenant, not the old, are a powerful reminder of the need to seek to walk in righteousness. He said, *"But as he which hath called you is holy, so be ye holy in all manner of conversation."*

This call to holiness should inspire and motivate us in our daily lives. We are saved by grace, to live by grace, so we can approach God boldly, as He desires to see us.

SHARPENING THE DULLER
SIDES OF THE IRON

*"Be shepherds of God's flock that is under your care,
watching over them—not because you must, but
because you are willing, as God wants you to be; not
pursuing dishonest gain, but eager to serve."*
1 Peter 5:2

We are created in God's likeness, and though our brokenness wrestles with it, each of us has a nature that desires to reach the heights those ahead of us have attained and exceeded. If humanity had been content with being stagnant, the creativity within us would have been buried, and the world wouldn't be where it is today. Think of it this way: if there were no teachers to train and equip us— whether in traditional schools or through other unconventional means—many things that make life easier for us to navigate would not exist: cars, airplanes, dishwashers, lawnmowers, etc.

As believers, we are all on a journey, and though we are each at different stages, Heaven is our goal. Every teacher is a learner, and there is always a step ahead of where we are. The value of having mentors can't be overstated; when we become content with where we are in our faith journey, the wisdom to learn by avoiding others' pitfalls and gaining momentum from their victories will elude us.

I know the world prides itself on the premise that *"We need to make our own mistakes."* While I agree to a degree, it is wiser to learn how to swim from a trainer than to jump into the ocean and drown. Michael Phelps did not become one of the greatest swimmers in the world by learning on his own. He had coaches who trained him over the years, and even with all his medals, he continued to train with the help of his coaches.

Proverbs 13:20 says, *"He that walks with wise men shall be wise: but a companion of fools shall be destroyed."* Wisdom is the key to growth. It thrives in a willing heart, and we grow faster when we hold the hands of those who have gone ahead of us. I owe my spiritual and personal growth to different mentors at various seasons of my life. Their wisdom has enlightened me, their histories have helped shape my history, and their love has strengthened my resolve.

I love the story of Jethro's advice to Moses in Exodus 18. Although Moses communed with God daily and was the primary point of contact between God and the Israelites, he needed to learn from others' experiences. This story teaches us the importance of humility and open-mindedness in learning from others, regardless of our status. With God's emphasis on specificity, one might think He would question Moses's decision to follow Jethro's advice, but He didn't. *Exodus 18:24* says, *"Moses listened to his father-in-law and did everything he said."*

If the Almighty God could say in *Isaiah 1:18,* *"Come now and let us reason together,"* how much more should we? Seeking people who can help us navigate the paths they have already walked is simple wisdom. Similarly, holding a friend's hand to caution them against falling off a cliff is the most Christian thing. No one can attain perfection until we cross to the other side of life, and so, at each point, we must ask questions of those who have already walked the path we are treading. We grow together in a synergy that revolves around constantly watching out for one another and sharpening the duller sides of our iron *(Proverbs 27:17).*

Dear Lord Jesus, thank you for who you are and for showing us how to live rightly on this side of Heaven. Thank you for the grace you've given us to be called children of God. I pray that you teach us the beauty of community and give us the wisdom to learn from those who can help us avoid the roadblocks ahead. Open our eyes to see the blessing of helping those coming behind us so that we might live in the fullness of your goodness. In Jesus's name, Amen!

SUSTAINABLY JOYFUL

"Praise the Lord, my soul; all my inmost being, praise his holy name. Praise the Lord, my soul, and forget not all his benefits." **Psalm 103:1-2**

Recently, I experienced a joyful high because something amazing happened to my family. I felt such a burst of joy when we got the news that I'd love to bottle up the moment and relive it every day. For a while, you'd think waking up with any more of life's questions or prayer requests was impossible. God had answered all my prayers instantly, and everything felt good enough for me to run a million miles for the Kingdom.

Well, not so fast. A few weeks later, I found myself asking God to help with this and that. I had almost totally forgotten that my bargain with Him was to listen to what He wanted me to do for others now that He had answered my prayers. He did His part and calmed my fears, which means

I should use the rest He gave me to bless the world and help His Kingdom come.

The human mind is often preoccupied with the needs of today and tomorrow. However, our gratitude tends to fade as soon as those needs are met. There is no such thing as reaching a level that guarantees continued joy outside of God. You can own the whole world, have the means to travel beyond the galaxies, and still feel empty. The joy that worldly achievements give you is momentary, not eternal. Only walking with God and living in His purpose for your life can make joy sustainable.

As I lay on my bed, I couldn't help but question my right to ask God for petty things when He had just shown up in such a big way. Like the Psalmist, I had to remind my soul to pause and remember God's goodness. I created a mental room for myself to live in—a room with walls filled with notes of remembrance of God's greatness. While I may still suffer from gratitude amnesia now and then, I am consciously demanding that my soul never forget.

Being sustainably joyful is a matter of posture and comes with intentionally reminding your soul who God is and His kindness toward you. He always comes through and brings us to the other side of the messiest roads. When you remove God as the source, everything crumbles; the formulas, hypotheses, and conjectures fall apart. Sustainable joy can only come from walking with the Most High, and enduring peace can only be found in Him.

UNCONDITIONALLY CHRIST'S

"Can anything ever separate us from Christ's love? Does it mean he no longer loves us if we have trouble or calamity, or are persecuted, or hungry, or destitute, or in danger, or threatened with death?" **Romans 8:35**

The best hour of my life was that afternoon when I placed my hands in the waiting hands of Jesus. Although my young heart had to weave through many curves to reach that point, it received grace from Calvary's stream. Since then, life has had meaning, and despite the many hurdles of each day, I am unrelentingly loved.

Christ's presence in your dark alley makes it a dancing ground, and His touch on your soul tingles your senses in the most precious ways. When you become a Christ follower, the world makes sense, and everything that was once blurry becomes clearer. It's like walking in a dark room all your life and suddenly having the light turned on. You hear, see, and feel in a way that nothing else in the world can make you do.

Although it will take a lifetime for your eyes to adjust to the glory of His majesty, His tenderness keeps you steady.

It's not where you were that determines the miracle; it's who you are currently walking with. You could have been a prostitute, a murderer, or a plain old religious girl like I was. Regardless of your circumstances, you are no longer alone from that moment on, and the weight once heavy on your soul becomes lighter **(Matthew 11:28).** Your response to the cross becomes the response to whatever you go through in life because the saving power of the cross becomes your daily help.

The world can question your choice to walk away from the dissatisfaction of your separation from God, but you know that what you once had is incomparable to what you received from Calvary. In verse 31 of **Romans 8**, Paul asked, *"What, then, shall we say in response to these things?"* He said that because he had tasted and seen the fullness of walking with Jesus and knew that nothing in this world compares to its satisfaction.

I am unconditionally Christ's. He is my help, my shield, my surety, my fortress, my King, and my Savior. I've been in the lows and highs of life and seen His presence, love, and faithfulness break through the thickest fog. At war, He fights for me; in the billows, He anchors me. To follow Christ is to be rested in the storm and to fight without lifting a limb because He gives His angels charge over me.

If I have to sit on the mountaintop, let me sit there with Christ; if I have to walk through the valley, let me walk through it with Christ; if I have to search in the dark, let me do so with Christ as my guide; if I have to choose a lamp, let its light shine on Christ. If I have to live, let me live with Christ; if I have to die, let me die in Christ.

JOURNEY THROUGH THE WAITING ROAD

"But now, for a brief moment, the Lord our God has been gracious in leaving us a remnant and giving us a firm place in his sanctuary, and so our God gives light to our eyes and a little relief in our bondage."
Ezra 9:8

I recently went through a long, winding waiting road. One thing is for sure: it's not fun walking it. The waiting road is always cloudy, and you can't see what's ahead of you. So, even if you only need one more step to reach its end, the proverbial light at the end of the tunnel remains blurry.

This time, each step along the path came with pain. I knew I had to keep moving, yet my weary heart told me I couldn't. I often lay awake at night, just praying for some relief from the mental strain of searching for that finish line that marks the end of my wait. My hope through it all came only from knowing who held my hand, and I found rest as I was wrapped in the arms of my Father.

Through that season, although long, God created rest areas along the path for me and gave me laughter, even when my situation said I shouldn't be laughing. I had moments when something would happen, or I'd receive some information to strengthen my resolve and refuel my empty tank. While those bright lights only lasted a few steps at a time along the long waiting road, they were reminders of God's faithfulness and His mindfulness of His dear child. They kept me moving and replaced my unbelief with hope. When that last curtain was pulled down, and I saw the finish line, I slumped into God's hands and simply worshipped.

God understands the power of hope and always finds a way to sprinkle it into dire situations. When in exile, Ezra heard of the people of Israel's unfaithfulness in following God, and he was distressed. **Ezra 9:3** says that he tore his tunic and cloak, pulled hair from his head and beard, and sat down appalled. It was a hopeless situation—not only were they in slavery, but they had also strayed from the laws of Moses, which set them apart from other nations.

Ezra prayed to God, knowing their sins had cost them their freedom. He acknowledged how God gave them moments of rest despite their exile. He said in **Ezra 9:8-9**, *"But now, for a brief moment, the Lord our God has been gracious in leaving us a remnant and giving us a firm place in His sanctuary, and so our God gives light to our eyes and a little relief in our bondage. Though we are slaves, our God has not forsaken us in our bondage."*

We all walk through the waiting road during different seasons of life; it's painful, I know. However, as dear children of the Almighty God, He always finds a way to shed His light and break through the cloud on our path. He provides rest areas when we think we can't take one more step. He reminds us that He is with us, that although our hearts are weary, with Him, we can make it through the dark and thorny terrains to reach the end of the road. We serve a God too faithful to leave us hanging in the balance, and He can never fail.

UNTIL WE SIT WITH JESUS

*"As they talked and discussed these things with each other, Jesus himself came up and walked along with them." **Luke 24:15***

Jesus, appearing to two disciples while walking to Emmaus, paints a picture of what walking with Him is like. Although He doesn't always show up physically because He's omnipresent, He is faithful to the end. Baffled by Jesus's question of why they were sad, Cleopas described Christ, "who is" right there with them, as one "who was" not there. He said, *"He was a prophet, powerful in word and deed before God and all the people"* **(Luke 24:19).**

Like Cleopas, we can't truly know Christ until we sit in communion with Him. Knowing Jesus means we are at the table with Him. It's not enough to know about Him; we must know Him to enjoy the peace of walking with Him. How sad it is to walk through life without realizing that Jesus is right beside you, walking with you. Imagine the joy the two disciples would have experienced if they'd realized they were walking with Jesus—they would have been spared hours of anguish. The Bible says their faces were downcast when Jesus first spoke to them because His crucifixion saddened them.

Amazingly, they seemed to know more about Jesus than Jesus Himself, yet they were too blind to see Him walking with them. Imagine someone telling your story to you when you've lived every second of it. They didn't hang on the cross; He did. They didn't go to Hell; He did. Even when He scolded them in **verse 25**, saying, *"How foolish you are, and how slow to believe,"* they still didn't catch a hint that it was Him. This experience shows that knowing the Bible does not equate to knowing Jesus, and having unpleasant memories of a church or some Christians acting up does not excuse our need for a Savior.

While we no longer have to guess or speak about Him in sorrow, many of us still live on yesterday's news about Jesus, declaring defeat on the cross instead of celebrating the victory of His resurrection. Christ is the risen King, and the secrets of the ages are revealed to those who call Him Father. Verse 13 of that chapter said it was intentional that Christ's identity was kept secret from the disciples, just as from those who had not accepted His invitation to the table.

We have to sit to see. Until the disciples sat at the table in communion with Christ, they didn't know Him. **Verse 31** says, *"Then their eyes were opened" during communion. Maybe they asked Him why He hadn't told them it was Him* *all along, and I'm guessing His reply would be, "I did."* Until they recognized Him, His words didn't mean much to them, nor did His presence.

Everything Jesus told them as they walked to Emmaus pointed to Him, but they didn't know. After the revelation, they said in **verse 32**, *"Were not our hearts burning within us while he talked with us on the road and opened the Scriptures to us?"* This is comforting because it shows Jesus' graciousness and patience with us. He'll keep trying; He doesn't push or shout; He keeps walking with us until we sit with Him. We must sit with Jesus, or anything we stand for will cloud our judgment and deny us the joy of living as sons and daughters of God.

THE HANDS OF JESUS

"Where can I go from your Spirit? Where can I flee from your presence? If I go up to the heavens, you are there; if I make my bed in the depths, you are there. If I rise on the wings of the dawn, if I settle on the far side of the sea, even there, your hand will guide me; your right hand will hold me fast."
Psalm 139:7-10

Holding hands are one of my husband's and my favorite things because they carry us through different seasons of life. Recently, I had the opportunity to teach my daughter the value of holding hands when she pulled hers away as I tried to hold it. I've always loved her tiny hands on mine, and I knew it was time for one of our little talks.

I explained the importance of placing our hands in trusted ones and what that symbolizes when we return home. It's a simple reminder that we are not alone, a way to express something meaningful without spoken words. From that moment on, we agreed that, no matter where we are, if she sees my hand, she must place hers in it—regardless of how dirty it is or who's watching.

Many of us walk through life, placing our hands in Christ's today and removing them tomorrow. We venture along paths, believing we know what we're doing, thinking we don't need to hold on to Him for the journey. We choose certain seasons of life to walk with Him and hold His hand, while in others, we think we can go it alone. We scramble in the dark, searching for a way out because, at some point, we let go of the hands of our Majesty.

No season of life is too messy for God to pull away from us. He is steadfast and won't let go when we surrender to Him. As David said in **Psalm 73:21-23,** *"When my heart was grieved and my spirit embittered, I was senseless and ignorant; I was a brute beast before you. Yet I am always with you; you hold me by my right hand."*

There is something genuinely comforting about holding hands. As simple as the gesture is, even in silence, it speaks volumes. It tells you that you are not alone, that the person next to you, holding your hand, is connected to your heart. It assures you that if you trip or fall, you have a helping hand to pull you back up.

Place your hands in the hands of Jesus, for how you respond to what life throws at you depends on whose hands you are holding. If your hands are in Jesus' hand when you walk through shallow waters, He'll keep you when you reach the deep ends. He'll carry you; in the dark, He'll be your guide; and when the sun shines, He'll shield you in His tabernacle.

GOD USES BROKEN PEOPLE, BUT...

"Not so with My servant Moses; He is faithful in all My house. I speak with him face to face, even plainly."
Numbers 12:7-8a

As a church, we must not allow ourselves to become complacent in sin under the guise of acceptable brokenness. Instead, we should encourage one another to seek God and repent of every sin. I, too, am guilty of this. I often take the path of finding solace by hiding my faults under the umbrella of my imperfections. But regardless of our beliefs, we must remember that God is holy and delights in using those whose hearts yearn for Him.

As I immerse myself in the stories of our spiritual ancestors, I am reminded not to glorify my brokenness but to ask God for help to rise above it. The phrase "God uses broken people" should not be a shield for our sins but a reminder of the transformative power of God's love. Our spiritual forebears, like David and Moses, were imperfect.

However, their actions were not driven by defiance in their brokenness but by their determination to please God despite human limitations. They were motivated by a deep understanding of God's holiness, which led them to experience intimacy with Him.

While they missed the mark and made mistakes, God knew their hearts and His history with them and corrected them. With all the wonders he accomplished with God, Moses walked in meekness and lived in awe of Yahweh. He served as a mediator between the Almighty and the people of Israel and never turned his back on God. Although he had a close relationship with Him, he did not take his access to God for granted.

There was just one Bathsheba experience in David's history because he needed only one to wake up. He writes in **Psalm 51:10,** *"Create in me a clean heart, O God; and renew a right spirit within me."* That sin did not become a pattern for him, nor did Moses murder another man after his first. They were not headstrong in their brokenness but allowed God to mend them through discipline and conviction. It didn't become perpetual for them to defile God's ordinances; they learned and repented.

God uses broken people, but not those who glory in their brokenness. When we do so, we are walking away from God, dragging His grace through the mud. The Bible does not say, *"Live broken,"* but rather, *"Be perfect."* That should be the standard we desire and seek. David repented and never repeated his sin, and Moses repented and was used by God. These people chose to honor God even when those around them forgot Him. We have a choice: to live in brokenness or grow in perfection.

LET JESUS MAKE YOU

"And He said unto them, follow me and I will make you..." **Matthew 4:19**

Think for just a minute, picture in your mind the number of people who have risen to stardom, loved by millions, praised by nations, and then fallen from their lofty heights. At some point in their lives, they feel on top of the world—untouchable and unmovable. It's as if the universe is at their beck and call due to the possessions gained through worldly approval. But when it all crashes, they find themselves relegated to oblivion.

So often, we get sucked into the tiny hole of crowd applause, ignoring the cautions of the only one who truly matters, Jesus. We pour all our resources into seeking people's approval instead of learning to live in honor of God. Friends we have today aren't guaranteed to hold that title tomorrow because worldly things often determine our value to them.

God is a master at turning ordinary people into extraordinary, history-changing humans. Those who stay with God until the end always emerge victorious. Their ending is always better than their beginning, as we experience ongoing transformation by walking with God.

Walking with God by following in Jesus' footsteps is rewarding because He elevates us from one level of glory to a higher one. As **2 Corinthians 3:18** says, *"But we all, with open face beholding as in a glass the glory of the Lord, are changed into the same image from glory to glory, even as by the Spirit of the Lord."* While change is inevitable when we carry our cross and follow Jesus, God celebrates every growth and gives grace for every mistake.

Let Jesus make you because if the world makes you, it can also break you. If Jesus makes you, they might shove, pull, bash, and oppose you, but they can't break you. A person who lives for God will die with a million gains, while a person who lives for a million gains will die with none. In God's hands, the ordinary becomes extraordinary, and even death is defined as gain, as Paul states in **Philippians 1:21**. Consequently, as a follower of Christ, you are eternally wealthy.

PART II

GROWING IN GRACE TO SAY 'NO'

"For the grace of God has appeared that offers salvation to all people. It teaches us to say "No" to ungodliness and worldly passions and to live self-controlled, upright, and godly lives in this present age." ***Titus 2:11-12***

There is more focus on the idea of saying "yes" in Christendom than on saying "no." Messages and books teach us to say yes to God and the needs of the Church. However, they don't often teach us that we must also say no to certain things to embrace God's call over our lives fully. Although everything may seem appropriate to pursue if it carries a Church or God tag, that doesn't necessarily mean it's right for you.

Like many Christians, I've run into trouble trying to take on multiple things without first asking God if I have the grace for them. Rather than asking before saying yes, I tend to agree first and then end up burnt out. God knows my heart and understands my passion for the kingdom, but I need to stay in my lane so I don't trip up others running the kingdom race. He is a God of order and distributes gifts to reflect His grace over our lives. Stepping outside that order or grace exposes us to challenges we aren't meant to face.

Saying no often brings the discomfort we associate with failure, especially when saying no to something good. However, saying yes to God sometimes means you must say no to many other things, even good things that fall outside the bounds of His call on your life. The grace for His children to accomplish anything comes from Him, not from our mortal minds or strength. Paul affirmed this in **2 Corinthians 12:9,** saying, *"But he said to me, 'My grace is sufficient for you, for my power is made perfect in weakness.'"*

We must understand the role God wants us to play and where He wants us to serve. We must also remain sensitive to the Holy Spirit's guidance and the release of grace. Without checking your *"grace meter"* before taking on a task, you might end up drained and hindered from fulfilling God's specific purpose for your life. Finding your rhythm in each assignment God entrusts to you will allow you to expand your role in kingdom work progressively.

TO LIVE LIKE CHRIST: JESUS IS JESUS.

*"Then Jesus said to the crowds and to his disciples:
"The teachers of the law and the Pharisees sit in
Moses' seat. So you must be careful to do everything
they tell you. But do not do what they do, for they do
not practice what they preach."* **Matthew 23:1-3**

I grew up eating only organic food because the world around me was not as industrialized as it is now. It's been years since then, and I still have difficulty adjusting to non-organic food tastes. While in terms of food, God has blessed humanity with the wisdom to maximize our available resources to combat hunger, I still like organic better because my mouth has tasted its goodness. For me, the pesticide and chemicalized lab versions don't just meet the quality of the originals.

The tendency to follow is ingrained in our mortality. While God created us as free thinkers with individual choices, He also made us to thrive in community. Before we look up, we mostly look around. We search for crowds we can blend in and be accepted into. People who look like us, talk like us, dress like us, and believe in what we believe. We clamor for leaders who speak to what we want and choose to listen to those we want to.

However, to live like Christ, we must learn from the source, not the sub-source. While you have to surround your life with mentors, pastors, godly friends, and families, constantly filter things through God's Word directly. You have as much right to learn from the Father as every Christian you know, and yes, that includes the most Christian human you know.

Many Christians have made idols out of humans because they can see God's gifts on display through them. Yes, you should honor and follow people who have walked the path you are treading, but do so cautiously, even as you read this and follow this page. I am not an authority; neither is anyone; God is, and we all have the same access to Him as followers of Christ.

Don't fall because your mentor's foot slipped or someone you've learned from disappointed you. Your salvation is yours, given by Christ, and is secured by the cross. Don't throw in the towel in defeat just because someone else has something to learn and grow from.

If we choose to live for Christ, we must also live like Christ. To do so, we must study Christ's life through the Bible and develop a thirst to know Him more than we will through Sunday morning sermons. You'll be amazed at how much you miss when you don't sit at His feet.

Your pastor, parents, or Christian friends might have the right idea and say the right things about Christ, but they are not Jesus; Jesus is Jesus. Learn from them, but model your life after Jesus, not them. As a human, He didn't fail nor falter because the Bible says, *"He knew no sin"* **2 Corinthians 5:21**. He already accomplished what we all struggle to achieve: perfection. However, the people around you are still in a process, so follow the person who has passed the tests.

In **Matthew 23**, Jesus encouraged the crowd to listen to what the Pharisees were teaching because they knew the scriptures. However, He warned against following them because they don't practice what they teach. Listening to the right thing is different from following what is wrong. Learning to separate both gives us and the people we are learning from the grace and room to fail—without taking us with them. This is because when they make things right with God, we might not be there to rise with them.

DON'T JUST SAY IT, LIVE IT

"That which was from the beginning, which we have heard, which we have seen with our eyes, which we have looked at and our hands have touched—this we proclaim concerning the Word of life." **1 John 1:1**

Don't just talk the talk; walk the walk. This is not directly from the scriptures but speaks from the heart of **James 1:22**, which says, *"But be doers of the word, and not hearers only, deceiving yourselves."* You definitely can't talk yourself into walking barefoot on a beach in Aruba while sitting in a house in Montana. And you most definitely cannot talk yourself into being a Christian without actively walking as a Christian.

Christ modeled Heaven's perfect example for us. He navigated complex, difficult scenarios and emerged unscathed at the other side of the curtain. He didn't hide in a crowd, assuming an identity that did not match how God had called us to live. He responded to unkindness with kindness, sinfulness with righteousness, pretense with boldness, and death with life.

The life that God called us to is full and satisfying, and we can't achieve it until we start living and minding how we live. While we are guaranteed safety in our redemption, we have to walk within the perimeters of that safety. Shouting commands without living the acts diminishes the efficacy of God's Word. If He says I can be holy, I must believe and accept it to walk in it. While I will not attain it in this life, I walk daily, pick my cross up, and venture to follow Jesus.

When John said, "That which was from the beginning," he was talking about Jesus and proclaimed that to live as He did is possible when we fellowship with the Trinity. Although we walk in the ocean of life with waves rising up and down around us, we must be mindful of who we are and the throne we represent.

To rightly affect our world how God wants us to, we must embrace godliness as more than a principle and make it a lifestyle. It's who we are and should be. To speak to what the world is doing wrong, we must first focus on what we need to do right. Many of us talk the talk without walking the walk. Our homes, children, work, actions, and reactions must reflect what the Bible says. We can't just be saying it without doing it. We know that God's truth will always be "the truth," but if we stop believing it, we will stop living it, and if we don't live it, we can't teach it.

IF YOU ARE WILLING AND OBEDIENT

*"If ye be willing and obedient, ye shall eat the good of the land." **Isaiah 1:19***

The journey of a million miles is said to start with the first step, and I agree. However, before that first step, something must move you within. It's easier to train someone willing to try than to force someone reluctant to make a move. They might respond to the lesson grudgingly and take one or two things away from it, but because their heart is not in it, they'll miss out on a lot more. If I knock on the door of your home, you must first be willing to let me in before you open the door for me. Responding to the sound of the bell does not equate to the willingness to let me in.

God has been teaching me about the power of a willing heart and how it is a requirement for me to accomplish the assignments He commits to my hands. I'm learning that it's a great place to start because God can do amazing things with it. To climb the ladder of maturity, I must first be willing to grow in obedience (**Isaiah 1:19**). I believe in God and know that without Him, I have no life, but my belief must move beyond that. I must be willing to do exactly what He tells me and go where He leads. A child forced to clean his room might do so out of obedience and not willingness. To walk in obedience, our actions must not be forced but from a willing heart.

My journey to the moment of writing this is one of constant tantrums. I say yes to God, but not until after searching for other ways I believe the chapter of my story should be written. Most times, I had to hit a roadblock before reluctantly handing Him the pen to draw the map for me to chart.

From lessons learned, I wait for prompts from the Holy Spirit before I jump on any train, even if it looks good. Although it seemed more sustainable and accessible until recently, I hadn't received the releases to have other writers write for "Abiding Christian." Maybe God wanted to grow my credibility in my reliance on Him or something else; I just knew I had to keep moving at the pace He guided me.

In verse 11 of **Isaiah 1,** God told the Israelites, *"To what purpose is the multitude of your sacrifices unto me?"* Sacrifice does not equal obedience; it's simply a response. The Israelites seem to know how to obey the ordinances but do so unwillingly, leading them to choose poorly. They believe in God yet constantly go against His will for them. Sacrifices without willing hearts do not move God because He sees through reluctance and carefree attitudes.

Some of my friends started writing articles that I did not byline a few weeks back, and their willingness to accept the challenge was humbling. It was not planned; I had a nudge, reached out to them, and they were just ready to go. They have blessed, encouraged, and strengthened believers they might never meet until we reach Heaven. The effect of their obedience to impacting the lives of many across the United States is tied to their willingness to allow God to use them on this platform as He has with me.

It doesn't take your readiness to surrender to God; it takes your willingness to surrender for you to be ready because we are perfected in the process of surrender. Like Moses, if you are willing to be the deliverer God called you to be, He will give you the rod to conquer Pharaoh. And like David, if you are willing to be the man/woman whose heart pants after God, He'll give you mighty companions to fight alongside you. However, you must go through the process.

EXTRAORDINARY DAUGHTERS OF GOD

"And many women were there beholding afar off, which followed Jesus from Galilee, ministering unto him." **Matthew 27:55**

The value of Christian women for kingdom growth cannot be overstated. Jesus knew this and made them integral in His ministry on earth. While the role of the twelve disciples formed the base camp from which Christianity grew, Christ's mission flourished because of the women who surrounded Him. Even in a culture that believed women should not play significant roles in important issues, God ensured they were an essential part of the story.

To start with, Mary was the first to know of the imminent visit of the Messiah to our broken world. God did not choose to tell an army of men or an earthly royal family first; He chose a woman. **Luke 1:28 says**, *"The angel came to her and said, "Greetings! The Lord has blessed you and is with you."* The privileged information of Christ's birth was given to a little girl with no strength other than her willingness to submit to the will of God.

Furthermore, during His short years of ministry, many women saw the glory of God in Christ and ministered to Him in different ways. Martha opened her home to and fed Him (**Luke 10:38**), Joanna sponsored Him financially (**Luke 8:3**), and Mary Magdalene washed His feet with her tears and lavished them with the oil in her alabaster jar (**Luke 7:37-38**). They loved Jesus and expressed it in the most tangible ways. **Luke 8:3** states, *"Joanna, the wife of Chuza, the manager of Herod's household; Susanna; and MANY others. These women were helping to support them out of their own means."* They were independently using what they had to support Christ's ministry.

The women were not just part of a crowd but actively followed Jesus. They played crucial roles in the grand scale of the events that led to this moment in humanity's history when millions call Jesus their Savior. They were not relegated to His background but essential to His purpose and journey to and after the cross.

Jesus trusted them because they were His friends. Yes, it was devasting to see Him on the cross as He went through the agony of death. However, even in their pain, they were Ministers of Christ. **Matthew 27:55 (KJV)** says, *"And many women were there beholding afar off, which followed Jesus from Galilee, ministering unto him."* Jesus was more than a hero lost in time to them; He was their Messiah, and they loved Him. After His resurrection, He appeared to them first, and many continued to live to honor Him. **Acts 9:36** says Dorcas did "Good things" and devoted her life to helping others because she was His disciple.

Being a woman of faith puts a level of gas in our pedal that accelerates the greatness within us, pushing us beyond expectations. We are not onlookers but participators. We are extraordinary beings, and the world experiences beautiful things when we walk in the fullness of who we are as daughters of the Almighty God. A woman who walks with God is called by love, established by grace, and lives purposefully in honor of Christ.

FOR ANOTHER DAY

"I will give thanks to the Lord because of his righteousness; I will sing the praises of the name of the Lord Most High." **Psalm 7:17**

The darkest place a man can be is a place void of God. A place where the vitality of the work of redemption accomplished on the cross at Calvary eludes the mind. A place saturated with the presence of self instead of the dominance of the Holy Spirit.

For all the reasons beyond man's definition, I am grateful for another day to wake up and call myself a daughter of God, a Zion princess, or, more importantly, God calls me His. While some days might be cloudier than others and the waves I'm riding on overly high, I stand amazed at the goodness of my Father. He is steadfast and faithful and holds me above all the moving parts of my life.

I am grateful that God counted me worthy in His grand plan for eternity to share His love with my world. He is one constant good in my life and the essence of every breath I take. The Psalmist said, in **Psalms 111:7-9**, *"The works of his hands are faithful and just; all his precepts are trustworthy. They are established forever and ever, enacted in faithfulness and uprightness. He provided redemption for his people; he ordained his covenant forever— holy and awesome is his name."*

While the world is far from perfect, and some days are downright too much to handle, I am grateful for all the things that warm my weary heart and give me a reason to reach for tomorrow. Despite all the shoves and pulls, God anchors me to the foundation of my redemption in Christ. But for God, there'll be no reason to hope, no trace of peace or place to hide.

CAUTIOUS GRACE

"What shall we say, then? Shall we go on sinning so that grace may increase? By no means! We are those who have died to sin; how can we live in it any longer?" **Romans 6:1-2**

We enjoy honey from bees, but bees also sting. Also, water is a source of life, but it can also take life, and fire is necessary for human sustenance and can also destroy. We cook and even warm our homes with fire but know not to stick our fingers in it; otherwise, it will burn them. Although all the things we need for life are accessible to humanity, they are also things that, if misused, can cause pain.

Grace lived right comes with a caution. To understand grace, we must embrace 'Caution' as a friend to keep us grace-aligned. Grace is not a pass to live as we like; it is an extension of God's goodness for us to enjoy all that pertains to life and godliness while honoring the sacrifice of Christ.

We are saved by grace and must live within the perimeters of grace as Christians. Writing to the **Ephesians**, Paul said in chapter **2:8**, *"For by grace are you saved through faith; and that not of yourselves: it is the gift of God."*

Just like God's grace for salvation, He also gives us different levels of grace as His children. To some, He gave the grace to preach, and to some, the grace for hospitality. However, many of us operate without cognizance of our perimeters and step out of the circle God destined us to be in. Whatever the grace God gives, it's paramount that we live within it to maximize His will for our lives.

I am guilty of stretching my tentacles beyond my limits, and I've had to pay the price for that many times. When I step outside God's grace over my life, it might be for something noble, but it always comes with heaviness. For instance, I have the grace to speak to Christians but not so much to politicians or people who have not crossed the line of salvation. If, for some reason, I step outside that grace, I will get drained by my actions so fast that I'll have to say, "Okay, Martha, back off; that's someone else's assignment."

Caution and grace seem to be counterintuitive, but they are actually complementary. Grace is a gift, and it's undeserved. One can say it is sentimental because it stimulates human emotions in the most beautiful ways if received correctly. If a stranger will give me his mansion on the condition that I manage it as long as he's away, and if I do, he promises me a better and permanent estate when he returns, I'll try my best to do that. I can't fault my benefactor if he doesn't trust me with the gift of a permanent home when he returns to find his mansion trashed.

Well, Jesus gave us new lives when we became Christians. He gave us the power to become sons and daughters of God (**John 1:12**). In addition to that, He also left us the Holy Spirit to help guide us through life. Caution demands that we live conscious of the Holy Spirit's leading and honor how Christ lived so we can pursue to live like Jesus. If we don't, we boldly abuse God's grace.

YOU CAN'T BLAME GOD

"When tempted, no one should say, "God is tempting me." For God cannot be tempted by evil, nor does he tempt anyone, but each person is tempted when they are dragged away by their own evil desire and enticed. Then, after desire has conceived, it gives birth to sin; and sin, when it is full-grown, gives birth to death." ***James 1:13-15***

My life has certainly not been a bed of roses, but neither has the life of anyone I know. I've not always made the right choices, and I don't know anyone who has either. You work through the earth's road, toiling to make ends meet, and you dare not blink; otherwise, you might lose it all. You work to nurture your relationships and stay above the waves so you don't get drowned in loneliness and emotional turmoil. If you ask the wealthiest among us if they believe they have everything they want and can sleep without worries, the answer is probably no.

This chain of demands puts every human at loggerheads with making the right choices for themselves while considering how it affects others. At some point, we do things that set other people up to trip, even when the intent is different. But this can lead to painful circumstances in your life or the lives of others. And while God is our maker and wants us to have the fullness of life, we fall short because of our broken nature.

It's easier to pile the loads of the misfortune of our broken humanity on God. Still, we can't blame God for the failure of man. **2 Peter 1:3** says, *"His divine power has given us everything required for life and godliness through the knowledge of him who called us by his own glory and goodness."* Our lives are a spiral of choices and, most times, interwoven with the intentions of others. Although there are a million and one unexplainable occurrences in our lives, most of our daily consequences are directly related to choices we or others make.

Trust me; there are days I want to wiggle my hands toward Heaven and point my accusatory fingers at God, screaming, why? Why did my father lose his job? Why did my brothers die? Why do I have to feel so much pain? Why does my life look blurry and more challenging than others? The lists go on, but so do God's patience, comfort, and mercy.

THIS LIFE I LIVE

"If we live, we live for the Lord; and if we die, we die for the Lord. So, whether we live or die, we belong to the Lord." **Romans 14:8**

People say life is precious, but how do we determine what 'precious' means? It is a relative word that can be interpreted differently. What is precious to one person might not be to another.

In chapter 14 of his letter to the Romans, Paul explains how to balance grace with truth and walk free of the guilt of condemnation. Although each Christian's life will differ, we are safe if we live rooted in Jesus. You don't keep a million-dollar diamond on the display table; you place it in a secured glass chamber where, although people can admire it, it's safe from mishandling and theft.

A life surrendered to Christ is shielded from destruction. Although people can see it on display, touch it, and it might even get a little smudge on it, if we allow Jesus to be the custodian of our life, He'll dust off the stains and secure us back on the stand. God's value for His children is worth more than a million diamonds, and the price tag on us is more than any human can pay.

Against the widespread belief that accumulation equals happiness, releasing your life to Christ brings rest and satisfaction. This is because true freedom comes from giving up what we hold dear to our hearts and allowing Christ to shepherd it. If I believe that my life is precious, the best place to keep it is in God's hands, and if I want someone to take care of my family, the best place to hide them is under the cross.

Even people who don't believe in God are living for something—if not themselves, then some ideologies. In verses 7-8, Paul writes, *"For none of us lives for ourselves alone, and none of us dies for ourselves alone. If we live, we live for the Lord, and if we die, we die for the Lord. So, whether we live or die, we belong to the Lord."*

While my feet still work, I want to run where God leads. While my hands can still move, I want to use them to point people to the cross and raise them to the Heavens. While my mouth can still make sounds, I want to speak of God's greatness and sing of His everlasting mercy. While my eyes can still see, I want to look at life through the lens of Christ crucified and see what He sees in people. While my heart still beats, I want every heave to resound Heaven's rhythm and every pant to be after God. While I live, I want my life to be hidden in Christ, my Lord.

IF YOU ARE READING ME

*"Looking unto Jesus, the author and finisher of our faith, who for the joy that was set before Him endured the cross, despising the shame, and has sat down at the right hand of the throne of God." **Hebrews 12:2***

Positive thinking is an idea filtered through the lens of mankind. It emphasizes the ability to believe and speak your beliefs into existence. Although it tries to mirror the positivity of the Christian faith, it is nothing like what the Bible teaches. While a positive thinking ideology promotes following one's heart and the power of self, a godly posture anchors on absolute surrender to God.

I am learning to read people better because, like everyone, I've fallen prey to judging books by their covers instead of their pages. I've come to understand that who you follow and what you believe are the core of who you are. The values and life system of someone who walks with Jesus rests on the premise that their life is not theirs but God's. They move at the pace of Heaven and, although still wrestling with human emotions, are more than the dictates of those emotions.

My expectations in a room of Christians are no longer misguided by human imperfections because that will always be constant. I am as human as anyone, so I know the struggles of keeping it together. It is now more about where we are in our walk with Christ and how far we are willing to go with Him.

Until we start reading the pages of other Christians' lives as finger-written by God, we'll miss the theme of the stories. It's a process, and we are all at different stages. We have the same theme, rooted in grace and mercy, and to see the accurate picture, we must read the story through God's eyes. Everyone is a work in progress, and the finale of all our stories ends in perfection—perfection guaranteed through our redemption and adoption into the family of God.

If you read me as the author of my life, you are misreading me. If you think I have moved an inch in the right direction without God, you're missing the entire point of my life. You are looking at the wrong picture if you can't see me beyond the patches of human imperfections. Lean in and look closer; you'll see that the pages of the final lines of each chapter of my life conclude in God's triumph.

Jesus is the author and the finisher of my life. He wrote the chapter on all my wins, smiles, laughter, joy, peace, mission, and vision. Every wrong thing in the story happened when I took the pen from Him and scribbled the lines. My life's greatest joy is knowing that I live for Christ alone.

HOW IS THAT WORKING OUT FOR YOU?

"But whoever drinks the water I give them will never thirst. Indeed, the water I give them will become in them a spring of water welling up to eternal life."
John 4:14

Thinking through a simple scenario... Two extremely thirsty men came across a well but could only draw from it one at a time. The first man went to the well and pulled his cup of refreshing water, quenching his thirst. After drinking water from the well, he went to his friend excitedly, telling him about his satisfaction. The friend looked at him and said he didn't believe there was water in the well and would not try to draw from it. He ignored the apparent change in his friend and dismissed his plea.

Looking at his dying friend, the satisfied man urged him to try getting his share of water from the well, citing he had nothing to lose by trying, but the friend refused. He had no alternative to quenching his thirst, yet he turned deaf ears to his friend's plea. We can all agree that it's not his friend's fault if the thirsty man dies because he was offered many opportunities to drink from the same well.

Wisdom demands that an empty, hopeless soul accept the gift of salvation Christ offers; if it doesn't, that's not God's fault. I would ask a thirsty man or woman who refuses to embrace the saving grace from Calvary's flow: "How is that working out for you?" Would you rather lose it all when you can have it all?

Lay your haughtiness aside and come to the well. A well that has continued to satisfy many spanning thousands of years is worth the try. Like the warriors of old and all the followers of the cross before me, I drank from it and am fully satisfied. Your pride or the money in your account cannot give you peace or buy you eternity. And your bitterness and belief in nothingness can never satisfy you. Don't die of thirst; draw from the well of life.

Jesus said, 'Whoever,' meaning 'anyone' who drinks the water He gives will never thirst again (**John 4:14**). Everyone falls into the category of anyone, and I urge you to draw from the gift of salvation Christ offers and see if you won't be filled. Think of it this way: You have nothing to lose trying Jesus but everything to lose if you don't give your heart a chance to encounter His Lordship.

TO KNOW THE LOVE OF CHRIST

*"And to know the love of Christ, which passes knowledge, that you might be filled with all the fulness of God." **Ephesian 3:19***

What does it mean "To know?" The phrase is so loosely used that even things that fall under guessing pass for "I know!" Knowing is a giant leap from what we think to what we know. It rides above the train of confusion and cannot be moved by innuendos.

If you ask a toddler learning how to read the ABC if they know it, you'll undoubtedly get the alphabet song in response. They will end with "Now I know," even if one or two letters got mixed up or he/she has no idea what they are used for. Knowing something is more than a half-baked truth with a few missing links. Knowing is either all or nothing. You must know to know, and there is no compromise. It means a deeply seated understanding that your knowledge is accurate and believed. It rests at the core of your existence beyond any doubt.

From a place of not understanding who Jesus was to become a champion of the faith, Paul understood the depth of Christ's love. This is seen in **Ephesians 2:19a**, "*And to know the love of Christ*." With his encounter with Jesus comes the knowledge of His love. Through his journey with Him, he knows that nothing he had experienced before, his wealth, education, and position, compares to the depth of Christ's love.

To know the love of Christ, you must take one step toward Him as Paul did and accept His offer of salvation. From then on, although not complete on this side of Heaven, you will be filled with all the fullness of God, that no one can pull you away from what you know to be absolute truth.

Knowing Jesus sips through every fiber of our being. It's inseparable or dilutable. The knowledge of Christ's love rests on the soul of the saved and gives an understanding of who God is. Through the outpouring of His love, we know God does not hold back His goodness. He is Gracious but not enabling, forgiving but not condoning, encouraging but not demanding, present but not encroaching. If you walk with Him, He completes you in every way.

FIXING THE PUZZLES

I was working on a puzzle my son made during his school's parents' conference, and although I got the first few pieces figured out fairly quickly, completing the puzzle on time before the meeting started wasn't easy. I didn't have a picture to guide me and had to rely on trying repeatedly to figure it out. It was somewhat frustrating because it took longer than I expected. No matter how often I tried to use the wrong piece, it didn't work until I connected all of them correctly.

Cornelius was a Pharisee, a leader, and a teacher of the scriptures, yet he didn't have the complete picture of life. He had the pieces but didn't know where to fix them. With his age and lifelong experience studying the scriptures, one would expect that he had it all figured out. However, he knew he needed Jesus to help him understand what it meant to follow God. He told Jesus in **John 3:2**, *"Rabbi, we know that thou art a teacher come from God: for no man can do these miracles that thou doest, except God be with him."*

Life is like a puzzle; putting the pieces together requires understanding what the finished picture should look like. No matter how we try to force the pieces into the wrong spots, we'll never get them right if it doesn't fit. It takes knowing God for life to make sense and following Christ to get the puzzles of life and eternity right. Until we reach that point where we acknowledge we need Christ to help us sort life out, we'll keep fixing life's pieces in the wrong spots.

Seeing the finished picture of my son's puzzle warmed my heart. It highlighted his goals for the school year, helping me know how to channel my efforts to support him in achieving his goals. When we don't know the accurate picture of our purpose, we'll run blind in life's race until we abandon what we know to learn what Christ knows. He was there when the world was made and has witnessed every occurrence in history. He sees the big picture and knows where each piece of our life goes. God will make the picture clearer when we trust Him with all the details.

PART III

ONLY POSSIBLE BY GOD

"How much more, then, will the blood of Christ, who through the eternal Spirit offered himself unblemished to God, cleanse our consciences from acts that lead to death so that we may serve the living God!"
Hebrews 9:14

Thinking about the complexity of humanity, the conflicts, divisions, and confusion make the simplicity of following Christ the one choice that gives meaning to life. You see, people make choices that seem impossible for even our mortal minds to fathom daily, yet we don't question the authenticity of their human nature. They steal, kill, maim, and destroy, yet they are one of us, no matter how cruel their actions are.

However, God has been consistently God, yet we question His existence. He made eternity before the beginning of time and the universe too vast to reach, yet we question His majesty. He has held this world together despite all our misgivings, yet we question the authenticity of His sovereignty. He gave up His majesty to walk among us and died cruelly at the end of His creations, yet we doubt His love. He offered forgiveness before we learn to conquer our sins, yet we question His mercy. He gives strength to the simple, yet we question His grace.

God does not have to do anything to prove Himself to humanity because everything already proves His wholesomeness. Our past, present, and future existence speaks to the authenticity of who He is. Without God, there will be no us; without Christ's cross and death, there would be no atonement for our sins. **Romans 5:6-7** says, "*You see, at just the right time, when we were still powerless, Christ died for the ungodly. Very rarely will anyone die for a righteous person, though for a good person, someone might possibly dare to die.*"

If I can accept that a man wicked enough to kill another man for his car or his wife shares the same human nature with me, I can absolutely accept that the peace and hope I feel deep inside me is only possible by God. I am created by Him, so I dare to live for Him. Although the authenticity of God's sovereignty speaks through the ages, and the beauty of His glory lines the width and depths of the earth, it speaks louder in my soul. And while the wonders of the galaxies sing His praise, all the fibers of my being where no one can reach or touch sing louder.

GOD, HUMANITY, AND THE BAD GUY

"The thief comes only to steal and kill and destroy; I have come that they may have life and have it to the full." **John 10:10**

W hen I think of the dynamics of the world, I see three players in the story: God, humanity, and the devil. God is always good; He loves humanity, and the devil is always on the opposite side, constantly trying to destroy humanity. Narrowing it down to these makes it easier to define things and assign them roles in everyday occurrences.

God is fully love-defined, and He is also a God of order because, in the absence of order, the devil quickly rears his ugly head. When He created humanity, He gave us the power to manage all He made before them. He prepared the world for us even before we got to the party. God told Adam and Eve in **Genesis 1: 29-30**, *"I give you every seed-bearing plant on the face of the whole earth and every tree that has* *fruit with seed in it. They will be yours for food. And to all the beasts of the earth and all the birds in the sky and all the creatures that move along the ground—everything that has the breath of life in it—I give every green plant for food." And it was so."*

We are not onlookers in the story of our existence; we are co-creators with God to nurture our world because God's creative nature is woven into every fiber of our being. God said in **Genesis 1:28**, *"Be fruitful and increase in number; fill the earth and subdue it. Rule over the fish in the sea and the birds in the sky and over every living creature that moves on the ground."* How we do that job determines how we enjoy the fruits from planting and harvesting times, and how we treat one another determines whether we live in peace or chaos. God is constant in His role, and unfortunately, so is the devil, but we humans are the flip-floppers, changing our allegiance and navigating life without heeding caution signs.

The role of God is written in love, spelled out with the blood of the Lord Jesus. He gives life, peace, joy, grace, and eternal rest. Speaking of Himself and countering the destructive agenda of the devil, Jesus said in **John 10:10**, *"The thief comes only to steal and kill and destroy; I have come that they may have life and have it to the full."*

Knowing these, as children of God, we are not unaware of the devil's devices. When bad things happen in our lives and the world, we know who is behind them, and when good things are happening, we also know who to thank for them because when we cooperate with the laws of life and godliness, God is committed to breathing life into all that concerns us. **2 Corinthians 2:11** states, *"So that Satan might not outwit us. For we are not unaware of his schemes."*

GROWTH IN QUIETNESS

*"For thus saith the Lord God, the Holy One of Israel; In returning and rest shall ye be saved; in quietness and in confidence shall be your strength: and ye would not." **Isaiah 30:15***

At the time I'm writing this, I feel overwhelmed. I can't say why or what the cause is, but my heart longs for that quiet space where the rhythm lines up with God. Do I have too much on my life's plate, or am I doing too much too soon? I don't know. I've committed my life to God's hands and ask that He use me however He deems fit. Yet I know there are times I step into something believing it would grow me, but it ends up draining me.

I've had similar experiences many times before and found that for my rest to be restored, I have to take a step back to sit at Christ's feet and allow Him to walk me through the things I need to let go of and the things I need to embrace. It's a place where trust takes over, pushing my worries and unrest out of the room to make way for Christ to lead. There, my rest is restored, and my burden is eased. It doesn't happen with the snap of a finger but with each puzzle piece moved to its rightful place.

There are seasons when we get into trouble because we step into too much and end up not getting anything but weariness. I have realized that it's not how many things you accomplish but how well you do the things God commits in your hands. God knows our capabilities, and for us to succeed at anything, we must ask Him before we step into any situation. **Isaiah 30:15** says, *"In returning and rest."* Even when you have a million things tugging on your shoulders, you must mind the one thing that truly matters: sit at Christ's feet to ask questions and be refreshed before you jump on the next wagon.

I continue to grow in quietness because, in it, I find rest. We can miss many important details about our life's assignments if we don't learn how to grow in quietness. Just because something is louder does not mean it's the right path. God walks us through seasons of quietness in different areas of our lives to grow us. Although He speaks in a still, small voice, He wants His words to be the loudest in our hearts. How we respond to His leading determines what we get out of life, and how we train our mind's ears determines how clearly we hear Him.

WHAT GOD HAS DONE

"And they overcame him by the blood of the Lamb, and by the word of their testimony." **Revelation 12:11**

There is a balance to living truthfully that we can't achieve by reasoning things out without the help of the Holy Spirit. Even something that sounds noble, like humility, might transmit pride if we don't engage the help of the Holy Spirit. Our neglect of boasting about the power that works in us (**Ephesians 3:20**) makes us come off as proud and arrogant people capable of changing ourselves. God did it, and when we don't celebrate it, we deny God's grace over our lives. Timothy writes, *"Having a form of godliness but denying the power thereof"* **2 Timothy 3:5.**

For instance, in the name of humility, we might fall prey to covering the power of Christ to transform our brokenness while hiding behind our 'strength.' An adulteress who has no desire to be what she once was because God changed her should sing her deliverance from the mountaintop. If she testifies to the power of the Holy Spirit in her, it's not pride; it's gratitude to God and His ability to take our messes and make beautiful things out of them. In doing this, she's telling other broken people, "If God did this for me, He would do the same for you."

One of my dad's favorite songs is "Go, tell it on the mountain." I can still hear his raspy voice singing it around the house. It's a song that urges us to be spreaders, not controllers of God's grace. God is Good; He is the Almighty, all-powerful, and He can do abundantly, above all, that we can ask or think (**Ephesians 3:20**), including overcoming our broken nature to walk in His fullness.

I'll be the first to acknowledge my broken humanity, but I must also be the first to boast about the transforming power of the cross. I am not the same person I was before I met Christ! While I still have spiritual and character wounds under surgery, I am already a new creature by virtue of my new birth. A transformation that sets me in the process of a complete overhaul through the washing of the Word. Like the creature Paul writes about in **2 Corinthians 2:17**, I can only be called 'new' because something new springs to life in me each time something old dies.

As I continue to bathe in the flowing river of grace, I celebrate every victory in my history because I owe it all to Jesus, my Savior. As a human, I still have many struggles and always will, but as a Child of God, continued triumph over my faulty nature is guaranteed. Like Paul said, "I die daily" (**1 Corinthians 15:31**). Daily death honors the work of Christ in me; it does not celebrate my brokenness.

Although it lurks in me, I smile and boldly declare that sin has no hold on me. I live by the power of my resurrected King, and while my battle against my humanity will only be fully won after my last breath, I am cloaked in the victories extended to me by Christ. As I do that, I'm telling the devil, "That battle is won; back off," and I'm also telling Jesus, " Dad, what's next to fix in me."

PEOPLE COME, PEOPLE GO, JESUS STAYS

"So we fix our eyes not on what is seen, but on what is unseen since what is seen is temporary, but what is unseen is eternal." **2 Corinthians 4:18**

If you are an adult, consider your favorite elementary school classroom. Remember your class teacher and classmates and the long hours you spend with them every weekday. It was like a season of life that would go on forever. Like me, you may have met a few best friends there and kept them through the years. Now, think of the possibility of getting everyone in your classroom together in one room again. The odds of that are slimmer than a few years after you all graduated because life has dispersed each person, making it almost impossible to pull off.

I have had the privilege of sharing life with some fantastic people, starting with my mother. Having gone through different educational systems up to graduate-level studies, I have become acquainted with people through my

84

journey. In addition, I've attended multiple churches, been part of numerous choir groups, and made many friends—and some non-friends in my short journey.

People come, people go, only Jesus stays. Think of the different great men and women this world has seen. Think of the phenomenon, battles, and victories in history. They are all relics on which time and season ride; they are temporal. No one man, innovation, or greatness outshines the glory of the rugged cross on which the Savior of the world was crucified. While victories can become defeat and yesterday's glories become withered grass, Jesus lives and reigns forever.

Many people I've crossed paths with are now remnants in my imagination, just as I am in most people's. As I journey on, I've walked away from people, and people have walked away from me. My presence in people's lives has been as inconsistent as theirs has been in mine. My mother and a few other people are gone, and I'm left scrambling to fill the vacuums people leave behind in my heart. At no point in each move I've made in life have I been able to transfer the same group of people and life routine, except my walk with Jesus.

Christ in us is the only treasure that can move from one season to another and then another. It is the only relationship that can last beyond a lifetime. He alone is the constant and consistent companion. A man who limits his mind from accepting the gift of eternity freely given by Christ denies himself the rest and joy from walking with a friend who never leaves. Although he/she might spend time here on Earth with a million people, they will come and go, but Christ remains.

HOW GOD SEES IT

"God saw all he had made, and it was perfect."
Genesis 1:31

The questions people wrestle with the most are, "How can God love the world with all the mess in it, and how can He die for unworthy people?" Although our mortal minds can never fathom the depth of God's love for humanity, we can experience it by accepting the gift of redemption through the death of Christ on the cross. **John 3:16** says, *"For God so loved the world, that he gave his only begotten Son, that whosoever believeth in him should not perish, but have everlasting life."*

How God saw His creation before sin entered the world in the Garden of Eden determined His response to us. We were loved before we knew what love was. On the sixth day, when God looked at the world, He saw perfection, not brokenness. He knew humanity's capabilities to flourish on Earth and the possibility of all scientific innovations.

Genesis 1 details the creation of the Heavens and the Earth, and verse 31 says, "Looking at everything, God saw all He created as good."

Everything on Earth speaks of God's goodness: the air, land, and waters. He was there before the lands were separated from the seas, and the first fruit dropped from a tree branch. When He created the universe, the plants were good, the animals were good, the seas were good, and man and woman were good. If He had seen it differently, His approach to the brokenness might have been different. To God, the world was worth dying for because although humanity made a mess of things, the blood of Jesus speaks better than the blood of Abel (**Hebrews 12:24**).

How we see things most often determines how we respond to them. If I see people as created in the image of and loved by God, I will respond to them with grace and truth. Grace implies letting them know that no one is too far gone from redemption. Truth implies letting them know that God is holy and wants us to walk on the path of righteousness.

If I see sin as a product of my brokenness, I'll respond to it remorsefully because I love my Father. If I see sin as an entitlement, I will ignore the nudge to ask the Holy Spirit to help me. I am training my eyes of understanding to adjust to the lens of God. Even if I can't see as clearly as looking through the windows of Heaven, I want my mind enlightened by the washing of God's word so I see and respond to everything as Christ would.

IF TIME COULD TALK

*"Be very careful, then, how you live—not as unwise but as wise, making the most of every opportunity because the days are evil." **Ephesians 5:15-16***

Naturally, what you spend the most time on determines what your life looks like. You can't spend time learning how to fish when you intend to become a great golfer or roll in the dumpster and expect to smell like roses. Also, you can't be heading to Heaven and spend so much time in places that do not glorify your destination. If we unpack the things in our life's baggage, we'll see that most things we've given priority to are counterproductive to all that pertains to life and godliness.

With the modern age comes the wave of information and different things vying for our attention. We are constantly pulled into situations that, if we consider them critically, do not contribute to the quality of life devoted to God and the kingdom. Life is indeed a gift and should be spent wisely because we are all accountable to the gift giver.

Many spend too much time shopping for life's values in the wrong stores, buying into ideas and things that consume us instead of improving us. We've rotated the "value clock" to focus on "me" in place of God and spend our lives browsing catalogs we should ignore and ignore what we should pay attention to. The prayer in **Psalm 90:12** asks that God teach us to number our days, yet we spend those days camped under the wrong tents. If time could talk, it would caution us, calling us out and sounding the alarm to position ourselves, ready to be used by God.

By dwelling place, in **chapter 90:1**, the Psalmist is saying that he lives conscious of God's presence, and when we do too, we'll be intentional about how and where we fill our treasure chest. You can't jump in every boat or enter every door just because you can. To be conscious of God requires you to go where He leads and move where He moves. While God's promise to never leave nor forsake us— endures till the end of the age, if we keep submitting our hearts and minds to things that do not glorify Him, we'll become less sensitive to His presence.

We are staying way too long in the aisles of life that only demand a pass-through. Until we stop doing that, we'll keep stacking trash instead of treasures. The world's version of the determination of quality time says, "Time is money," and God's version says, "Live wisely." Every second spent pouring into things that do not improve our quality of life and the lives of those around us is time wasted. As we pursue the things of God, our life's worth is heightened, and time begins to answer to us.

THE GOD-ANGLE TO LIFE

"Listen to my instruction and be wise; do not disregard it." **Proverbs 8:33**

When the nurses handed me my daughter, and I saw her in the delivery room, gratitude and love washed over me. Looking at her face and feeling her delicate body, I had no idea how to clean a tiny human, let alone raise one. However, almost two decades later, God's Word has been the road map through which my husband and I have navigated, and it's proved to be enough.

We chose the God-angle from the start, and while we might have made many mistakes, God's grace is sufficient as we continue to learn from Him. If you still ask me how to raise a child today, I'll point you to Christ because only through His grace have I been able to do things correctly. Although we are blessed to have help along the way and find comfort in walking with others as we journey through life, God's counsel is better than that of an assembly of the wisest humans in a hall.

To get it right in everything we do, we must look at it from God's angle and trust Him to take it from there. A man who honors the rules of the game has a greater chance of winning the gold than one who does not. How we love, act, react, and even raise our children should mimic the heart of God, regardless of negating forces.

Why give away wisdom to embrace uncertainties? What value is a bag of nothing compared to a bag of treasures? Living wisely is to walk within the confines of life in honor of God. God's love is all-encompassing, and His eye-view is beyond our minds' view. We can't go wrong trusting Him because He knows what's ahead of us and how to help us navigate life.

God's ways work because every detail is written in truth that unfolds in His love for humanity through Christ's death. A million ideas have come and gone, but the precepts and wisdom of the Bible are eternal. Instead of looking for detours around the Bible, learning to live by it will save us a lifetime of brokenness.

THE SOUND OF HOME

"And I heard a sound from heaven like the roar of rushing waters and like a loud peal of thunder. The sound I heard was like that of harpists playing their harps." **Revelation 14:2**

My dad loved country music and often listened to Jimmy Reeves, Kenny Rogers, and other country legends. Although it's been decades since I was a child in my parents' home, if I hear Jimmy Reeves's voice singing on the radio, it will send my heart pumping faster, transporting me back to my childhood. It is not Jimmy's voice that captivates my memory; it's the feeling of home that pulls me back to the confines of the walls where I once found refuge and unwavering love.

I am not one to be insensitive to the pain that the sound of a home might bring to some people. While hearing an old country song can warm my heart, it wasn't always cozy in my childhood home. One such difficult season was Mum's periodic sickness, creating moments when my little heart didn't know how to manage the anxiety that came with that. However, that was still my cherished and loving home, and the memory of my younger, stronger Dad, sitting on his chair listening to his records, gives me great comfort.

My friend recently told me, talking about her parents, "I miss being a child in their home." I could almost touch the beauty of her experience as she spoke, and it warmed my heart. Something about living there to this day still gives her strength to hope and fight for that experience for her children.

As Christians, when we keep our eyes on Heaven, we experience the joy and peace of home despite the draining noise in our world. With that same consciousness, we get accustomed to the voice of Christ to guide us through life. In the uproar, His voice will keep us calm, and when the noise in your head wants to drown you, His voice will keep you afloat. The sound of Heaven is a sound of peace, and it mutes all anxiety knocking on our heart's doors. **Psalm 85:8** says, *"I will listen to what God the Lord says; he promises peace to his people, his faithful servants."*

When I close my eyes in worship, I hear the sound of Heaven from beyond a billion galaxies far away, yet it echoes so close to my soul that I can't help but quiver. While it sizzles through the gushing of the winds and roar of the mighty waters, it sounds sweeter than anything on earth, cutting through every inch of my existence to give my weary heart rest. John describes what he heard in **Revelations 14:2** as *"The rushing of waters and a loud peal of thunder."* The sound of home, beyond the melody of the host of Heaven, is the voice of my Father. I can't see but hear Him as He calls me out of the murky wells life throws me in, and He surrounds me with peace in the face of adversity.

GOD'S PROMISES AND OUR RESPONSIBILITIES

"Your kingdom is an everlasting kingdom, and your dominion endures through all generations. The Lord is trustworthy in all he promises and faithful in all he does." **Psalm 145:13**

God is trustworthy, and His promises are the bedrock on which we flourish and the air with which we ride on the wings of hope. Without them, there is no faith, and Christianity would be an empty box. God's promises cover all that pertains to the life and godliness of His children. Our journey starts with the promise of forgiveness and culminates in a life of asking in hope for our daily bread as we walk toward our promised home in Heaven.

We bought a book of God's promises for our children when they were younger, and they read it before they went to bed each night. It was a little book with different titles that started with "God promises to..." I can still hear my daughter's voice reading it; "God promises never to leave me, God promises to provide for me, God promises to lead me, etc. Years after, those words still ring in my ears. Remembering God's promises gives our life meaning and makes navigating it more explicit, knowing there is a bright light at the end of each tunnel. It's so important for all of us to remember.

I love the Bible because it is the story of a good God filled with promises of courage and strength for any weary traveler needing a reminder of God's unrelenting love. I love all of God's promises, even those that convict me. I live daily with my heart and soul hanging on God's faithfulness to His promises. The walls of my home are filled with them, and my heart affirms them because I've seen them come through for me many times.

However, with God's promises come our responsibilities, and while He is committed to His side of the bargain, it does not excuse our responsibilities. We might have to get our hands dirty to eat the fruits from a blessed garden or burn a pinky to bake the best bread. When God says, "I am your Jehovah Jireh," it does not mean you sit in one room and expect to be fed modern manna from Heaven. While He is committed to His promise to provide for you, you still have to work, and He'll bless that. The bottom line is that you participate in the process of God fulfilling His promise for your life.

Our responsibility demands that we learn to fight before we get in the ring; if not, we'll be knocked out with the first punch. Learn to swim before we jump into an ocean; otherwise, we'll drown. When God instructs us about what He wants to do through us, the duty lies with us to follow the path. If God says you are to write to bless His people, you must learn what you need for the assignment: get a degree, read more, and get a mentor. If He says you will be an employer, you must learn to lead and master the trade He commits in your hands. God's promises are everlasting, but to experience them, we must live with a sense of responsibility.

THE SPECIFICITY OF WALKING WITH GOD

"I will instruct you and teach you in the way you should go; I will counsel you with my loving eye on you." **Psalm 32:8**

G od is not lazy and has not industrialized the process of creation. We are each made intricately by the Master, and our story has the undivided attention and care of the Sovereign God. He does not use the human model of "One size fits all" but instead approaches our lives on the premise of specificity. Although we walk on the same narrow road, there are instructions along the path we tread that are specific to us.

If you've been following Abiding Christian, you'll know my mum. She is my best example of Christianity because I saw her walk with God in good times and through dark valleys. As her daughter, I saw that Jesus never left her through each turn, nor did she throw in the towel when the road got too bumpy. He was her friend, strength, comforter, and Father, and I love the God of my mother.

In my thirty-plus years in Nigeria, I never saw my mum wear jewelry. The reason for that was not out of self-righteous piety but out of obedience. She said she loved gold so much that she spent hours traveling to other states to buy earrings and necklaces. They had a hold on her heart. On the morning of my brother's naming ceremony, she said she was upstairs getting ready when she received direct instruction from God not to use jewelry again because it affected her focus on God.

One would expect that someone with such an encounter would discourage all her girls from using jewelry, but she didn't. She told me that she'd never buy me jewelry, because she doesn't go near them, but Dad could. She said the instruction was for her and not us, and when we grow up and can buy them for ourselves, we are free to.

It's easy for us to generalize and mistake God's specific instructions. Walking with God comes with foundational principles that govern the redemptive soul. But in between the chapters of each of our stories are lines drawn peculiar to our journey. For instance, all Christians must love their neighbors as themselves, but God determines how we express that love. Just because one Christian mows the lawns of His neighbor does not make it a rule for all Christians because the love expression of another might be to pray for his neighbors.

Although they might look different, we can serve and express God's love in our highs and lows, regardless of who or where we are. Abraham served God as a citizen and as an alien; David served God as a shepherd and king; Moses served God as a desolate and a Prophet. We can show people Christ's love from any cultural perspective and any position we occupy. Although written in the same Book of Life with the same Blood of the Lamb, the specificity of our assignments' details speaks to our hearts' health.

From my Mum's approach to her walk with God, I learned that to fulfill God's assignments, I must listen and understand what God wants to teach me and apply them to my life. I don't mind if He's giving others the same or different instructions. I need to obey mine before I can help others.

FEELING GOOD IN GOD'S GOODNESS

*"Let us not become weary in doing good, for at the proper time, we will reap a harvest if we do not give up." **Genesis 6:9***

In Genesis, after God created the Heavens and the Earth, the Bible says, "*God saw all that he had made, and it was very good."* **Genesis, 1:31.** I can only imagine the fuzzy feeling in God's heart when He saw His goodness on display. He made the birds in the sky and the fishes in the sea and made man rule over everything. He saw the green in the fields, the brightness of the sun, and the shades of blue in the firmament, and He saw that they were all good.

There are two forces at work in the world, whether intended or unintended. Our actions are responses to either of them. Understanding this helps us navigate our choices better. God will never applaud evil, and the devil will never celebrate good. To honor God, it must look like God and reflect His love, truth, and grace. While there are times when

God will caution us to hold off on something we believe to be right, it doesn't mean He discourages good; it might just not be our assignment or the right time to do it.

Acknowledging the intricacies surrounding doing good, helping, giving, and just showing up, the question is, "Who will this make happy, God or the devil?" If I can settle that it warms my Father's heart, I'm okay, even if it costs me some discomfort. It might be painful, but at least it made God happy and put a dent in the devil's ride. Some people's happiness comes from hurting and taking away from others. As Christians, deriving joy in walking in love reflects God's nature embedded in us; joy in God's goodness is our heritage.

While it's imperative for us always to remember that because something looks and sounds good, it does not mean it is God-approved, it's also important to know that you can't go wrong walking in God's love. You are permitted to feel good for doing something that honors God because God is good, and our soul responds to Him.

GOD'S SIDE OF THE STORY

"Why do the heathen rage, and the people imagine a vain thing? The kings of the earth set themselves, and the rulers take counsel together, against the Lord, and against his anointed, saying, let us break their bands asunder, and cast away their cords from us. He that sitteth in the heavens shall laugh: the Lord shall have them in derision." **Psalm 2:1-4**

I know we have our scientific explanations for why humans continue to dominate over other creatures, but even science acknowledges that what God said about humankind prevails. Have you ever wondered (forget science, I mean, personally) why majestic creatures like the dinosaurs that once existed are now extinct, yet humans live on? While science gives us different theories behind the eradication of these giants that once dominated Earth, the fact remains they once were, and now they are no more. Through fossils, we can't deny they once lived where we now call home.

God defined us as rulers, and we've continued to be just that. When He made man and woman, it was with the intent of fellowship and to rule over all the things He made (**Genesis 1:26-29**). We continue to live out that charge despite our denial of His sovereignty. I know that because of the seeming continuous growth of science and innovations, our haughtiness toward our creator balloons, but the undeniable is that the more we know, the more questions we have.

God's side of the story is rooted in love, grace, and truth. When humanity fell, our limitations unraveled because although we continue to dominate the Universe and rule over all creatures, our lifeline to eternal peace remains in our view of and walk with God. Despite our defiance, He sent Jesus as the atonement for reconciliation, yet we rebel. Although He speaks through times and seasons, the galaxies, firmament, and even the air we breathe, we question His sovereignty.

The idea that we can put God in a court of man's laws to question His existence or dominance is laughable. **Psalm 2:4 says**, *"He that sitteth in the heavens shall laugh,"* at the myopic delusion of His creatures. Our minds have become so limited that our eyes govern what we believe to the despair of our weary souls. Although it stomps the mind that there is such a thing as a million lightyears, we believe it because we can see it through a telescope. However, our hearts are closed to God, whom the **Psalmist** said in **34:18** is *"near (enough) to the brokenhearted and saves those who are crushed in the spirit."*

God loves us and will accept us back to communion with Him, no matter how far from Him we've walked. Jesus said in **John 10:10**, *"...I have come that they might have life and that they might have it more abundantly."* It's a choice we all have to make to accept Christ and believe in God or live in our desolate bubble.

PART IV

MISSIONAL CHRISTIAN: IT STARTS IN JERUSALEM

"And ye shall be witnesses unto me both in Jerusalem, and in all Judaea, and Samaria, and unto the uttermost part of the earth." **Acts 1:8b**

When we hear the word 'missions,' the first picture that comes to mind is most likely a malnourished child from a village in an economically challenged part of the world. It's not the revival crowd that once defined the word. Thank God for the missionaries He sends to remote parts of the continents and for the hope He gives people in difficult places! People willing to answer the call to leave their nations to go to other nations are heroes of our faith.

I sincerely believe that global missionaries have a special place in Heaven because of their sacrifices. And in honor of those sacrifices and those who lay down their lives daily for the cross, our comfort level as Christians should be challenged. While it's important to be Christ's hands and

109

feet, we must not forget the holes in those hands as He hung on the cross and why He did it. He died to save everyone and wants them to have eternal life, and it's our responsibility to go and tell them.

We don't get to live in the fullness of godliness without a level of grit and sacrifice, even right where we are. They say health is wealth, and that applies also to spirituality. Don't get me wrong—God wants us to feed the hungry, clothe the naked, and empower the powerless—but equating material wealth to spiritual health is deceptive. Take a short walk in your neighborhood or turn on your television, and you'll see the dire need for Jesus where you are.

I'm a staunch advocate for God to send missionaries to the West because they're losing the steam God wants the Church to live by. Americans need Jesus just as much as any pagan nation does. When I tell people I am a missionary living in America, they seem confused because they believe missions are tied to earthly needs and that since the country does not need people from other countries for health or welfare, I must be mistaken. However, Jesus said we should be witnesses (it's about the gospel), and while we can accompany that goal with food, water, and healthcare, the core (100%) is the gospel.

Every Christian needs to ask God what He wants them to do for missions right where they are, in Jerusalem, before asking what He needs them to do in Judea. Witnessing Christ must start where we are before God can trust us to move beyond our borders for specific assignments. Even Jesus started His ministry within His borders in Israel.

I did leave my home country to live in the US, and as a Christian, I must be kingdom-minded because if God brought me here, I must live here as a missionary. The narrative that it takes being poor to need Jesus is sending the wrong message and making many Christians lackadaisical in minding the spiritual wounds in their and other people's faith. It's making us narrow the gospel and redefine Jesus's call to be witnesses.

We must start prioritizing maximizing people's gifts and leveraging them for local mission purposes, teaching them to live like missionaries at work, school, and neighborhoods. Evangelize! This Christian movement started in Jerusalem (**Acts 2**), the home base of the disciples, and we can't ignore ours.

If God instructs you to go to a foreign land, please go, and if He says to stay, don't take that as "I need to fold my hands and relax." There is so much to do with so little time, and the Kingdom can use you. Let the builders build, the singers sing, the writers write, and the teachers teach. Just live 'missionally.' Our witnessing begins where we are because if you can't shout it in Jerusalem, you cannot echo it in Samaria.

They sure do not need Western missionaries in Lagos, where I grew up, because we already have many churches and faith banner bearers serving the Kingdom. We had at least five churches on my street alone, and my home Church holds four services each Sunday in an auditorium that seats fifty thousand people and an overflow that seats even more. A fifteen-year-old born-again Christian in Nigeria can pray for hours at a night vigil, while an adult American Christian won't want to miss her beauty sleep for that.

If anything, I miss the vibrancy of Christianity I grew up with, the boldness, tenacity, and faith, and I pray daily for Christians in the nation I live in now to encounter God the same way I did. I want my children to see the power behind the gospel; it's more than a cozy feeling. I dare you to spend a month with a devoted Christian family in Africa and pray when they pray, go to Church when they go to Church, read your Bible when they pick theirs, and see if your spirit won't be energized.

While Christians in underdeveloped nations would welcome the hands of love from afar, they need us to be strong in our faith, holding the fort in this part of the world. We can encourage them through intentionality by not masking our need to raise our children to walk with God, pray, and read the Bible. As Christians, the mission field is anywhere people need to hear about Christ Jesus; hence, every school, street, and workplace needs it. If you see the same thing I'm looking at when you walk the streets, you can't deny that the need is much, even in our immediate neighborhoods. If we place all our hands on the strongholds and push against the walls of darkness together, the light will rush in, dissipating it.

Yes, Jesus did say to go to the uttermost part of the earth, but before that, He said to start in Jerusalem and Judea, and our Jerusalem is here, where we are. We are leaving too many margins that can cause weariness for the coming generation to continue to fight the good fight of faith. No matter how well-dressed your neighbor or coworker is, if they don't know Jesus, they are poorer than a penniless Christ follower living in a mud hut in a third-world country.

True witnesses of the cross live on missions daily, everywhere they go. We are all called to serve and be a light to our families, friends, neighbors, citizens, and the people we interact with daily. Tell them what Jesus is doing in your life, about eternity, and the need for them to accept His call to salvation. How we live matters, and so does how we serve. We can't ignore the darkness because whether people are rich or poor, live in Europe or Asia, the same rules apply to all; every dying soul needs Jesus.

Until we understand God's purpose and calling and live consciously by them, we'll miss out on daily opportunities to be witnesses. While some are privileged to go on or are called to global missions, many Christians will never travel beyond the shores of their nations, but that doesn't mean they hang their witness hat. So, use your gifts where you are as long as they point people to Jesus. We are all called to minister to the people around us. Our fulfillment in life lies in knowing what role God wants us to play on the world's stage and actively living it to witness Jesus.

GET UP AND GO TO CHURCH

"Let us rejoice and shout for joy! Let us give Him glory and honor, for the marriage of the Lamb has come [at last], and His bride (the redeemed) has prepared herself." **Revelation 19:7**

I live in a society that has become complacent in its approach to the community of believers, which is one of the greatest blessings of our faith. Where I grew up, the church played a vital role in the edification of Christianity, and it was evident. Despite the uproar and diverse challenges in the country, Christians are thriving, and the Church is joyful and growing. Oh, the joy of the Church in Nigeria!

This mental shift of the relative need to attend Church in the West stems from the gradual pull to shrug off the necessity of the Church as a spiritual life source. It demands that everything be rosy, physically comfortable, and suit our schedule. An entitled mentality that believes our presence in

Church is to favor God rather than the expectation that God blesses us with His presence when we are in church.

Sadly, many believers have allowed their minds to travel down this patchy path, forgetting that the beauty of our salvation rests at the foot of the bloody, messy cross of Christ. The road to Calvary wasn't pretty, so the rhythm doesn't always have to sound like the chorus of angels, and the children's church does not have to fit our preferred theme of "Alice in Wonderland." The Church is an assembly and not a club. Think of the upper room, where the first church gathered, and let that encourage your resolve to always be in church.

You don't stop eating because you had a bad experience at a particular restaurant. I'm also sure you didn't give up on food just because one spoonful had a weird taste last year. Why, then, do you allow the devil to steal your primary source of peace and joy by convincing you to stop drawing from the portion of salvation enjoyed only in the Church? You can only experience the fullness of life in Jesus, and only in Him can you truly live in your true identity. This experience comes from fellowshipping with other Christians, so go to CHURCH!

As a believer, I've been privileged to attend a few churches in the past few decades. If I had to travel the world, it wouldn't be to see the ruins or pride of the nations, but to visit churches as a partaker of the blessing of fellowship. I chose my first church outside my family when I was born again in the early 1990s. The church went through a difficult season a few years in, and almost all the churches I've attended since have also had challenges. However, to reduce the overwhelming sense of love from accepting Christ to the comfort we should always have in our local Church means denying the gravity of what Calvary represents. As a rule, my husband and I have resolved to stand by the church except if we are fully convinced by God, not being spiritually fed well, or for spiritual or biblical errors. It must never be, "For comfort's sake."

For decades, the Church has been my most comfortable place and a source of mental serenity because I get to experience Heaven each time I sit among fellow believers. Besides being with my family, it still is. This does not mean there are not times when I felt like pulling a few stands of hair out of my head because of my discomfort with how some things are done, how a leader acts, or how a believer in church behaves. However, I'm sure I'm not on the favorite list of some brethren at church either, and that's completely fine because it's all part of the growth process that prepares us for eternity.

We must understand that our reason for attending church goes deeper than 'how it makes us feel.' It's rooted beyond the sentimentality of enjoying the right worship melody or attitude from other worshippers. It's an appointment where God meets with a group of believers He is eternally committed to. Jesus loves His church and calls her His bride. Why won't you want to be consistently present in church?

Additionally, attending the local church is not negotiable if you want to live fully in God's plan for His people. Instead of planning church around every other activity, plan your activities, including vacations around the church. We tell our kids this because being at church reminds us of what home (Heaven) will be like.

Inconsistency in attending your local assembly to "If We Can" denies you and your children the joy of partaking in His feast. And in this glorious feast, Jesus is committed to showing up to serve when we gather. This doesn't mean God's presence isn't with you at home, work, and on the streets; it's just different. It's tied to our call to obey **Hebrews 10:25**, *"Not forsaking the assembling of ourselves together, as the manner of some is; but exhorting one another: and so much the more, as ye see the day approaching."* My family is so accustomed to friends we sit around at church that we notice when they are absent. They are family.

When next you choose to snooze an extra hour to miss church, remember the millions in the 'Underground church' who would give anything to worship in your place. It's a privilege, not an entitlement. And the excuse that a member of the church you attended eighty years ago offended you isn't a valid excuse for you to miss church. Change your place of worship if you have to; just get up and go to church. It's your Father's house, and because He still loves you, allow Him to serve you the goodness He makes available during corporate worship.

WHERE ARE THE WONDERS?

"And the Lord looked upon him, and said, go in this thy might, and thou shalt save Israel from the hand of the Midianites: have not I sent thee?" **Judges 6:14**

When the angel of the Lord appeared to Gideon in **Judges 6:12-22**, he was shocked by the title bestowed on him (A warrior). Although all that Gideon could see was his people's troubles, God saw a deliverer in him. I can imagine the smirk on Gideon's face, saying, "Pardon me, my Lord, but if the Lord is with us, why have all these things happened to us? Where are all the wonders?"

His identity as a warrior wasn't captured in his expectation of saving his people until God opened his eyes. He had all the excuses to discourage God from sending him: 'You should have done it; my tribe is weak; prove that you are the Lord,' he thought. Gideon's misunderstanding of God's character led him to expect God to resolve the situation single-handedly. However, he failed to realize that God often works through men, using them as extensions of

His divine will. This realization is a powerful reminder that we can also be instruments of God's work.

Like Gideon, many Christians sit around daily expecting thunder to roar over the unjust and angels to appear and shepherd the lost physically. What can a little 'I' do on the grand scale of the world's demands, we think? We've convinced ourselves we are too insignificant to make a difference until God reminds us that our willingness to extend a hand commits His outstretched arms.

Did you notice what God said in **Judges 6:14**? He told Gideon to go "*In his might*" because his potential was enough for God to do great things. God uses people not because they have the ability to push a mountain but because they are willing to put their hands on the mountain. For every miracle that got the Israelites out of Egypt, there was a Moses, and for victory in the battle against the Midianites, there had to be a Gideon to lead the chosen 300.

Step out of the hiding place, waiting for a revival. It's already here because you are here. Each time you point a finger at God for a miracle, four fingers point back to you.

You are the wonder the world is anticipating because your redemption earns you strength and courage in the likeness of the heroes of our faith. It gives power and boldness to your feeble hands, enlarging your weary heart. As you look to God for answers to the pain in the world, live in the consciousness of your identity: a wonder through whom God wants to save souls, feed the hungry, fight injustice, and lead an army out of hell to the throne of grace.

EVEN THE THINGS I CAN SEE

"For even if there are so-called gods, whether in heaven or on earth (as indeed there are many "gods" and many "lords"), yet for us, there is but one God, the Father, from whom all things came and for whom we live; and there is but one Lord, Jesus Christ, through whom all things came and through whom we live." ***1 Corinthians 8:5-6.***

Looking in the mirror, I saw a woman staring back at me, but the longer I looked, the less sense it made. It prompted me to ask, "Who or what am I?" Yes, I could see the beautiful black woman staring back, but those are just definitions given to me by a world that can't resolve the stirring in my soul. I've lived with this woman all my life, been everywhere she's been, and felt every joy and pain she has known, but until I allow my heart to think of God and my soul to wander in His love, nothing about me makes sense. I am created in the image of God, the Father who, although I've not physically seen, gives meaning to my being beyond what I could see in a man-made mirror.

Many things we can see, touch, taste, and feel don't make sense: the world, the galaxies, the unexplained and explained phenomena, and the simple intricacy of the human heart baffles us. Without God in the mix of any formula we stir together, it always turns out wrong and flat, leaving us with more complicated questions. If you look long enough at yourself in the mirror, you'll reach a point of dilemma because beyond the features staring back at you is a soul that longs for something more than the world can satisfy, but God can. To truly understand the intricacies of knowing who you are, you must first know and walk with Jesus.

The more I think of myself without God, the less sense my existence makes. Such an attempt thrusts my mind into an endless chasm of darkness because it leaves me existing and not living, with more questions than answers and without purpose. However, the more I fix my gaze on Jesus, the clearer things become and the more meaningful life is. My soul finds rest, and my heart is filled with an unspeakable joy. I can almost touch the glory of my life when I think of myself in the context of God.

In **1 Corinthians 8:5,** Paul concluded, "*There is one God, the Father, from whom all things flow.*" That knowledge comes from a privileged depth that only those who accept Jesus can access. The place of rest for my restless soul is knowing that 'I am' Martha, a wife, a mother, a woman, a living being created by and for the pleasure of the' I AM' God Almighty.

WHEN DEBORAH AROSE

"Villagers in Israel would not fight; they held back until I, Deborah, arose, until I arose, a mother in Israel."
Judges 5:7

As was their habit; after enjoying peace for eighty years because of a leader who feared God, the Israelites returned to their old ways, abandoning God's laws given to them through Moses. **Judges 4:1** says, *"Again the Israelites did evil in the eyes of the Lord, now that Ehud was dead."* Their disobedience led them into oppression until they cried to God for help again.

The story of Deborah unfolds at a time when her people desperately needed a righteous leader, someone with unwavering courage and strength in God to guide them out of their self-imposed captivity. She was not just a wife or mother but a prophet and warrior. Her unwavering faith in God and deep understanding of her role as His child guided her leadership. She led, judged the people, and settled their disputes with wisdom and courage.

Her presence on the battlefield reminded the army of Israel of God's strength. The Bible said the villagers held back and would not fight until Deborah arose—so much that Barak told her in **Judges 4:8**, *"If you go with me, I will go; but if you don't go with me, I won't go."* Her intention was to triumph with God's help, not to compete with the men. She was on the battlefield with Barak, yet she cared for his honor. Her people found solace in her walk with God, which was a refuge for the mighty men who surrounded her.

The confidence with which she said, *"Until I, Deborah, arose, until I arose, a mother in Israel,"* is rooted in a deep understanding of her identity. As I read this story, my spirit jumps with excitement because I walk this path and rub shoulders with many Deborahs waiting to arise from slumber and take their place on the Kingdom field. They are strong daughters of Zion just waiting to be stirred, women whose sole purpose for existence is to live to honor Jesus. They are doctors, lawyers, teachers, engineers, nurses, mothers, and wives—women ready to worship in the wasted places of their nations and join in the battle to restore them.

The virtuous woman in us is alive and well, but for restoration, God wants Deborah to rise. Her nation stood with God when Deborah arose, and the men were encouraged. Just like Deborah, the world eagerly awaits women of faith to step beyond the shallow waters and dive deeper into the things of God: pray, fast, study, evangelize, and love like Christ.

We are vessels in the hands of a master sculptor, created to restore hope as we abide under the shadow of God's wings. In embracing our identity, we will ignite the powers within us to fight for our nations, homes, marriages, sons, and daughters. There are many of us, which means the world cannot overcome or defeat us.

There is a Deborah in each of us, and I speak to them in their hiding places. I pray in the name of Jesus that there will be a stirring in the hearts of every woman who reads this, and our inner being will be strengthened to fight like warriors. Together, by the strength of the Most High, we rise above the waves holding us back from living in the fullness of our purpose in God: restorers and builders of wasted places. I pray that with God's hands guiding us, we will push beyond the walls the world has built around us, united in our mission to make Kingdom impacts for Christ's sake. Amen!

PURSUIT OF RIGHTEOUSNESS

*"For the grace of God has appeared that offers salvation to all people. It teaches us to say "No" to ungodliness and worldly passions and to live self-controlled, upright, and godly lives in this present age." **Titus 2:11-12**.*

It seems impossible to live in righteousness in our world today, where everything seems acceptable, yet nothing makes sense. When you think you've seen the worst things, something happens that dwarfs the mountain of wickedness, injustice, and immorality you previously witnessed. Every day comes with the desperate cry of God's elect to Heaven, praying for the grace to live right in a world clouding our understanding of right and wrong.

The jumbled definition of living right has left many scratching their heads. Our pride and self-imposed glory put us at odds with God's sovereignty, and the closer He draws close to us, the farther we move away from His call to live godly lives. We have convinced ourselves that the righteous God, who gave up His own Son for the sins of mankind, will have to live with our lack of remorse and dirt.

We cannot achieve Godliness by our own strength and good works. It takes the grace of God to choose right over wrong at every moment of our life here on earth. It is a daily adventure ride on the wings of grace. **Titus 2:11** says that God's grace, which offers salvation, teaches us to say "No." And it is only by that grace that we can stand, consistent in our pursuit of righteousness, regardless of our challenges in this world.

Denying ungodliness is not a one-time deal but a consistent evaluation of each moment of our life, weighing our decisions, actions, and reactions on the scale of God's word. Saying no when God says no and yes when God says yes. Leaving no decision for our corrupt mortal minds to decide but sifting the norms through Heaven's filter and looking at everything through the lens of Christ's sacrifice on the cross.

WHAT GOD SAID IS...

*"The Lord says, "I will guide you along the best pathway for your life. I will advise you and watch over you." **Psalm 32:8***

Like many Christians, after my salvation, I expected a wave of the wand to disperse all my troubles. My bags were packed for a long journey, vacationing with Jesus. I was sure I would start riding on a boat without waves under it or clouds above it. I misinterpreted the satisfaction my soul felt at the moment I accepted Christ as a ticket to live without another tug at my heart or attack on my life. I was ready to live in the clouds and not shed a single tear till I die.

After taking a few steps into the race, I realized my misconception. Although my hope was steadfast and my joy was unabated in most ways, it was definitely not a ride without storms. I prayed for my sick mother and expected instant healing and got none; I asked for an ovation for choosing a life devoted to growing in Christ but got an uproar instead. As I looked closer, I saw war raging all around me and realized the miracles of my salvation were more than what man could give me. It was the joy, peace, hope, grace, honor, and strength I had when I thought I could not take one more step.

Being saved doesn't entail that God will extract us from the battlefield; It commits Him to fight for us on the battlefield. It's His presence that makes the difference. God stands by His Word, like the certainty of the air that keeps us breathing. The role He plays in the lives of His children, although convoluted by man's misconceptions, can't be more forthright. God promises to guide us through the best path in life and is a present Father who never leaves. He is constant in and out of seasons, regardless of the height, depth, width, or magnitude of our life challenges.

Don't believe the lies; God might not explicitly speak to His children frequently; however, He always guides us with His loving-kindness (Psalm 32:8). However, for our souls to hear God clearer, we must reduce the volume of the familiar voices in our heads to be conscious of His presence. You might even need to change the dial of the compass with which you live because your predetermined conclusion might not be God's perfect will for you. God's word must always sound like God, not a man-made version of God. Even amid a battle, His voice will bring peace to your heart and soul. He will remind you of the magnitude of His love through the death of Christ and sprinkle on you the hope and pleasure that comes from walking with the Most High.

GROWING IN PERFECTION

*"He told them another parable: "The kingdom of heaven is like a mustard seed, which a man took and planted in his field. Though it is the smallest of all seeds, yet when it grows, it is the largest of garden plants and becomes a tree so that the birds come and perch in its branches." **Matthew 13:31-32***

I wouldn't say I liked going outside at night when we lived close to a forest because an Iroko tree was a few miles away from my parents' house. The tree rose above the hills and spread its branches over surrounding trees. Despite the distance, it towered over all the other trees in the forest; it was terrifying. It was high and wide and lived up to its name. Knowing the myth behind the Iroko tree in Yoruba land and seeing its majestic stance wasn't helpful. It overshadowed the other trees in the forest, and my young mind feared it.

In the parable of the mustard seed, Jesus compared the Kingdom of Heaven to this little seed. He explained that the unassuming, tiny seed becomes the largest tree in the garden. Although it would look unimpressive in its infancy, as soon as it gains root and sprouts its first branch, it becomes a mustard tree, a force to be reckoned with in the league of trees.

Although most Iroko trees existed for years before my birth, and I've never seen one planted, it's fair to assume that, like the mustard tree, every living thing has a starting point. What I could see beyond my house did not become massive in a day; it grew into it. It was once a little tree trying to live up to its name as the king of the forest.

Before a tree became a refuge, providing shade, it was a seed. As a child of God, you are on a journey to becoming a resting place for your generation. Just because you don't look like what God promised yet does not mean God is not working His perfection in you.

As Christians, we are not growing to be perfect; we are growing *IN* perfection because the nature of Jesus already makes us perfect. A day-old *Iroko* tree, just like the mustard tree, is called an *Iroko* from the day it was planted, and as believers, we are declared perfect the day we become Christians. However, even an Iroko can be uprooted, so as long as we stay rooted in Jesus, we will continue to grow in perfection because His perfection defines our destiny.

BEYOND ONE WONDER ARE A BILLION MORE

"For the earth shall be filled with the knowledge of the glory of the Lord, as the waters cover the sea."
Habakkuk 2:14

Having my home state witness the awe and wonder of the recent total eclipse is a privilege that will remain with my family for a long time. It's one of those events that cause such a big buzz, and you think it won't be worth it, and then you are blown away by the gravity of amazement you experience. It's worth more than every T-shirt, banner, and gadget made to celebrate it. As much as I hate traveling, I will travel a thousand minutes to witness one minute of it again. It was amazing!

When we packed the picnic bag and left for the park, we thought sitting outside for two hours, watching the gradual covering of the sun by a dark circle, would quickly bore us. However, as soon as I looked up, I didn't want to look back down because my soul was captivated by the wonder of the heavens. It was beyond my expectations and kept my heart transfixed. Even the kids were mesmerized by how closely we participated in the majesty of God. How anyone can see that and not revere the greatness of God is sad.

Looking up to see the eclipse sent my mind running, and the wonders beyond this one event gripped me. How can you not see the finger of God in this? We've become so oblivion to our spirituality that while we need specialized glasses to see the eclipse, there are different phenomena around us that we ignore.

Behind the about ninety-three-million-mile distance of the sun, the glory of God speaks daily, but because we sleep and wake up to them, we've lost the awe to stop and look. God's love and creativity speak through every living thing, great or small, through the sky and seas. Millions of stars light the sky at night, and the ocean's vastness holds whales and creatures beyond our imagination. We breathe in the air we can't see and witness the dawn and breaking of each day, yet those have become insignificant instead of phenomenal.

I am grateful for the privilege of having stood still with millions of people worldwide as we looked to the sky to see God's glory through the eclipse. At least, it made us all look up and remember that God can still amaze us in wonder. However, beyond that, my heart is renewed to see the immaculate craftsmanship of His work in things I've become so accustomed to and take for granted as an entitlement.

As the Heavens declare His glory (**Psalm 19:1**), I bow my soul in honor of my creator and proclaim His splendor above all I can see, feel, and touch. I don't have to wait another twenty years or travel through space to remember who God is and the extent of His love for humanity because the evidence is all around me. God is majesty personified, and a billion eclipses cannot compare to His glory. A simple beat of my heart reminds me of Him, and the bloom of the roses births a fire in my soul to worship Him.

HOW CAN I NOT CHOOSE CHRIST?

*"Peace I leave with you; my peace I give you. I do not give to you as the world gives. Do not let your hearts be troubled, and do not be afraid." **John 14:27***

As I flipped from one TV channel to another, the conversations threw jabs at my heart. It felt like the world would lose its footing the next minute. I was so overwhelmed that I just muted it. I studied journalism, so I know its effect on shaping how we think. What I heard were conflict-driven, life-sapping, and hope-depriving. For a moment, I thought, how can the world know peace when we've made humans our source without acknowledging the Kingship of Christ? After all, He is the only Prince of Peace (**Isaiah 9:6**).

The choice would be easy if we objectively weigh the options of walking with Christ alone or following the world's dictate. I believe peace has been and still is the scarcest human emotion. We'll pay anything to spend just a day with peace. Nations sign peace treaties that hang in the balance of being shredded, and homes built on love sometimes turn into battlegrounds despite marriage agreements. Because of our pride, humanity has tilted the balance of its existence to rely on our impoverished minds, creating constant chaos in our lives and the world.

With the wisdom dominant in me by virtue of salvation and as a creation of a good God, I chose Christ daily because He first chose me. Christ offers peace, and the world offers chaos. The world says I should have a million reasons to fear, and Christ says I have a single reason to enjoy peace: "Follow me." When I ride on the waves, He says He'll be my peace, and when giants face me, He says He'll fight for me.

Fear may live at my doorstep because I live in a chaotic world, but I have the key to my mind in my hands and choose to lock it out. Everything in life speaks to the brokenness and limitations of my humanity: fear, anxiety, envy, impatience, and a long list of discomfort. However, everything about my redemption speaks to the possibility of me being an extraordinary being created for the sole purpose of living for God. With the satisfaction of being His child, how can I not choose Christ when the alternatives lack peace, righteousness, joy, and hope in this life and eternity?

JESUS, I, AND WRITING CHRISTIAN

"And the Lord answered me, and said, Write the vision, and make it plain upon tables, that he may run that readeth it." **Habakkuk 2:2**

If you were in Church on Sunday morning at Christian Heritage Church (CHC) in Tallahassee, Florida, in 2011, you'd visibly see how terrified I was to be called out by a visiting Pastor whom Pastor Ron McCants, our Senior pastor, had invited. I can worship undisturbed in the presence of a billion people; however, standing alone with the minister in the presence of a few hundred people is a different story. I was familiar with several eyes that stared at me, but the situation was still uncomfortable. I had just stepped down the stage after ministering in the choir and was mortified when the preacher said he wanted me to come before the entire Church to deliver a message God wanted me to hear.

I picked up my first writing pad when I was young but didn't know it got Heaven's attention. While I wrote a lot in my teenage years, I thought I would be a lawyer. I would write about things happening around me, and I even remember the titles of my first two articles: "It is Good to Be Good" and "It is Bad to Be Bad." Simple, because two neighbors inspired it; you guessed it, one was kind, and the other was not. I always had this unexplainable urge to write to encourage or share what I was learning through writing.

Standing in the presence of many witnesses in the church that day made it impossible for me to shake off or forget God's assignment. I have loved my Savior and have not abandoned my love for writing. However, I didn't know how "Writing for the Church" would fit into 'my plans.'

While derailing to start "Stars of Afrika" in 2016, I felt a burden in my heart, telling me that it wasn't God's will for my life and nudging me to take my Christian writing seriously. I thought continuing to share my thoughts on my social media would compensate for the restlessness, but it didn't. To figure out how to navigate my assignment, I'd inform every Church I attended of my availability when I started, but that also had curtains limiting how the light filters through. So, I jumped on a wagon with Jesus, deactivated my social media, devoted most of my time to Christian writing, and eventually started "Abiding Christian."

Knowing that the church is a community of believers, I obeyed God's order and reached out to the appropriate people at the church. I set up meetings with pastors and leaders to inquire how to serve. My usual pitch is, "I can write; don't pay me; just let me know what you need me to do."

The process was often uncomfortable but necessary as God walked me through training seasons. I grew (still growing), learned (still learning), and persevered. Getting here, I have been privileged to learn and work with some amazing Christian writers. People who showed me the possibilities of using our gifts to reach the world beyond the walls and confines of our Church.

They strengthened my faith and determination to walk with God. Now, my eyes are turned to the heavens, and the warrior seed planted in me by God speaks loud in how I proclaim my faith: bold, audacious, and relentless. My simple measuring scale is "If it doesn't sound like God, it can't stay; it has to go."

I became intentional in seeking quietness, reevaluated my priorities, and deactivated my social media for five years to fully focus on learning to listen without distractions. I was willing to shut out any noise with God so He could manifest in and through me. It took months to get to that point of surrender to publish weekly because the thought was daunting, but God's grace had an unending flow I didn't know was possible.

It's been over twenty years since I sat in that auditorium under the voice of Pastor Myles Munroe, and "Die empty" still re-echoes in my ears. Although it's not been all roses and ocean breeze, God is holding my hands. Even when I don't want to hear it, my husband says daily, "From your home, you'll be impacting the world for Christ." God intends us to spread our gifts on earth, not haul them back to Him, and like you, I still have too much inside. There might be many oppositions, but God, through earthly guardians, continually holds me up every step of the way.

I was comfortable on my personal social media because I was familiar with my audience. God had to shake that by using a clean slate to build "Abiding Christian." In His usual manner of growing His children, now that I'm comfortable in my discomfort, God is moving me to another growth process of discomfort. What that looks like, I'm not sure.

God is hunting for Christian creators to speak life to a dying world and reach the ends of the earth with the message of love, grace, and righteousness through salvation in Christ Jesus. We live in a digital age, and the Church has not fully captured these gifts and is not maximizing them for the massive demand on the mission field. God needs an army, but there are few laborers (**Matthew 9:37**).

God went the extra mile by sending me many witnesses to ensure I stayed on course and did not give up; I can't fail Him. I don't know what seeds God has placed in you, but please nurture them and surround yourself with people who will help water and fuel the fire, not diffuse it. Even if it doesn't look like much, don't give up because God is committed.

Writing is a ministry, and without a mic in hand, in obedience and surrender, God will continue to reach thousands of people with the message of hope in Jesus and rattle those who still need Him. It didn't start when I published the first article or was called out in front of the church. The journey began with the willing heart of a young Christian girl living in a brown house on a street in Lagos, Nigeria.

My resolve is in God's faithfulness, and I see it continuing until I take my last breath and hand the baton to whoever God wants me to be. More treasures are in this mud, and I follow God's leading. He saw something in that little heart of mine decades ago and said, "I can work with that." I trust Him! At this stage of my life, I may still have a mile or a billion to go, but let it be that every step I take is where Jesus leads.

WOUNDED FOR OUR WOUNDED SOULS

"When Jesus heard this, He told them, "Those who are well don't need a doctor, but the sick do need one. I didn't come to call the righteous, but sinners."
Mark 2:17

It is hard to think of perfection in the world we live in today. Each time we flip through our news feed, something is tugging at our heart's core. There are wars around us, and injustice in our human systems is a daily struggle. The evil permeating people's hearts is unimaginable, forcing us to ask, "How does this end?"

Our world is so lopsided that we only need to look in the mirror to see her utter brokenness. Despite the constant pursuit of self-satisfaction, nothing feels good enough. We can adorn our lusty flesh with all its demands and still feel empty. The more we fill in, the emptier we feel.

The fall of man in the Garden of Eden left our souls wounded. It left us longing for insatiable material needs to replace the satisfaction of communing with our Heavenly Father. While we can complement our earthly desires with worldly gains, the core of humanity links our soul to the creator. And until the soul of every man finds healing through the thirty-nine stripes of Christ's suffering, the longing for satisfaction will never cease.

As deteriorated as today's world, it was not so in the beginning. In **Genesis 1:31a**, the Bible states, *"God saw all that he had made, and it was very good."* God made the world a perfect place, and man was the perfect icing on the cake made by a perfect God.

It's easy for us to get caught up in the earthly benefits of walking with God (Sound health and provisions), and we forget that our overall prosperity hinges on the health of our souls (**3 John 2**). Jesus exchanged His beautiful scars for our wounded souls and died to restore humanity to God. The gravity of this truth is evident in the fact that God didn't have to come down to set the Israelites free in Egypt, nor did He have to die to make King David one of the wealthiest men that ever lived. But He needed to abandon Heaven to die for our sins and restore our relationship with Him. **Isaiah 53:5** states, *"But He was wounded for our transgressions, He was bruised for our iniquities…. and by His stripes, we were healed."*

The crucifixion of Christ is the ultimate sacrifice, and the walk to Golgotha measures beyond anything, even our ability to live well here on Earth. Although there are stories of healing and blessings in the pages of the scriptures before the birth of Christ, the story of redemption was completed on the cross at Calvary. The death of Christ marks the end of our struggle to return to God and the beginning of the eternal fellowship that connects our souls to our maker.

WHEN A CHAMPION SPEAKS

"For the Lord your God is the one who goes with you to fight for you against your enemies to give you victory." **Deuteronomy 20:4**

If you've heard a champion speak, you'll see and hear the confidence that can only come from a place of certainty of victory. The voice may be calm, yet everyone listens because it resonates. This is especially true after a race or battle is won. I am not referring to the weightless, proud noise from an empty cymbal but a declaration of strength from one who knows exactly what he/she is talking about.

A champion might have sore limbs or even a bloody nose as evidence of a brutal fight, but that does not stop him/her from talking from the place of victory. Being a winner gives you an edge over your opponent because you are at peace knowing the fight's outcome. Although you hurt from the punches and falls, you expect they'll heal again.

As Christians, the battle is not ours; it belongs to God. We know who wins before we even step into the arena to fight. While we are not promised a battle-free life, God declares us champions, and as such, we should project the spirit and speak like it. Certainly, our hearts and bodies might get a few bruises to prove we've been on the battlefield, but our souls cannot be crushed.

God's command to His people in **Deuteronomy 20:1** is, *"When you go to war against your enemies and see horses and chariots and an army greater than yours, do not be afraid of them, because the Lord your God, who brought you up out of Egypt, will be with you."* How awesome is it to know the score of a match before it even starts? God promised victory, and He is as committed to fulfilling His Word today as He was in the days of old.

The salvation clarion does not call us to live in denial of the battles raised against us; Jesus wants us to know about them when He said, *"Be of good cheer, for I have overcome the world"* in **John 16:33.** God's assured presence makes the difference in the lives of believers because instead of fighting alone, He fights for us. **Isaiah 43:2** says, *"When you pass through the waters, I will be with you; when you pass through the rivers, they will not sweep over you; when you pass through fire, you will not be burned."* If you walk with Jesus, your victory is as sure as the "Day and night that will not cease." Genesis 8:22

We live defeated when we don't know the strength of the God who fights for us, believing that the bruises and bumps we sustain in the fight are signs of defeat when they are simply battle scars. Just because the enemy threw a few lucky punches does not mean he wins. As you get to know God and understand the power of being His child, you'll approach life's battles differently. The strain will hurt, but they can't destroy you. You are always a winner because no matter how many times you fall, you'll be the last man/woman standing, and the last one standing speaks like a champion.

PART V

GOD'S LOVE DEFINES YOU

"Before I formed you in the womb, I knew you; before you were born, I set you apart; I appointed you as a prophet to the nations." **Jeremiah 1:5**

I was reading about "The Coat of Many Colors" recently, and it was fascinating to see that while the coat played a massive role in it, there was more to that love story. The story is about Joseph and his father's love for him before and after the coat. **Genesis 37:3** says, *"Now Israel loved Joseph more than any of his sons because he had been born to him in his old age."* Joseph has been loved from the day he was born, even when Jacob thought he was dead. When his other sons and daughter tried to console him in **Genesis 37:35**, he told them he'd mourn his son's death until he died.

I've read these verses repeatedly, and like many people, I place so much more value on the coat than the lessons the story teaches about love. Love is undoubtedly expressive, but love does not start or end with material things. The coat's value is not in its beauty because it does not define love alone; the heart behind it is the value. While it expresses Jacob's love for Joseph, his love for him is not defined by it.

To walk in love, we must know what, or in this case, who love is. **John 4:8** says, *"Anyone who does not love does not know God because God is love."* We can't exhaustively define love because it's impossible to define God; God defines us because God is love.

The coat of many colors symbolized Jacob's love for his son, but the coat was destructible. However, just because Joseph was stripped of his coat did not diminish Jacob's love for him. He was broken by the thought of his son's death, not the bloody fabric returned by his other sons.

Until we stop living a lie that God can grow out of love for us, we will not fully grasp the depth of Christ's love for us. He is persistent and constant in His love, and His death on the cross proves it. While God enjoys lavishing His children with goodness, sound health and mind, and riches, they are not your value. Like Jacob's love for Joseph, God's love is indestructible and abounds beyond what we can see.

The devil is a master of deception and often deceives God's children by attaching the value God places on us to material things. This sometimes makes us put so much value on God's expression of love for us that we forget that even if we lose everything He blesses us with, His love remains constant. The material and social things I enjoy are God's gifts, but I live aware that those things express His love for me but do not define it; His heart defines it.

JESUS IN THE ROOM

"When one of the Pharisees invited Jesus to have dinner with him, he went to the Pharisee's house and reclined at the table." **Luke 7:36**

Envision Jesus in the room you are in right now. Think of Him sitting before you, hanging out in your space, just like He did at a Pharisee's house in **Luke 7**. The thought, although intriguing, is intimidating. The questions going through my mind are: what do I do, and how should I act? Should I sit, stand, smile, or be still? Should I bow, or should I look in His face? Do I turn off the television or choose a Jesus-appropriate program to watch?

Having Jesus physically visible in the room is too much for me to grasp until I think of Him relaxing in Martha's house and a Pharisee's house. What a blessing that we have the Bible! While elevated above the universe and clothed with unfathomable glory, Jesus's visit to Earth removes the ambiguities of His ability to understand our humanity. He is God and was fully man for thirty-three years on Earth.

Although daunting to think of it visibly, I have experienced Jesus in the room many times, alone and with other Christians. I'm presently experiencing Him as I write this article. Writing about Jesus means I think about Him a lot, and I almost always want to know His opinion on every thought on my mind. While I acknowledge that I believe in His omnipresence (Always there), there are those moments you can feel Him in the room, to the point of heart-pounding.

When you live in the consciousness of Jesus in the room, you are sure of stillness in the uproar, shelter in the storm, shield from the battles, and grace to rise again. He doesn't walk out on you because you need to tidy up; He helps you clean up and gives newness to each day with strength for your life's 'to-dos.' His presence in the room makes Heaven closer and mountains like dust.

If you are a Christian and want to enjoy Jesus in the room, make worship a constant activity in your space. Although it won't hurt, it doesn't have to be on for twenty-four hours; just let your space know He owns it. It releases an aura of peace and tranquility even when things seem upside down.

THE INEXHAUSTIBLE TOPIC OF GOD

"And I pray that you, being rooted and established in love, may have power, together with all the Lord's holy people, to grasp how wide and long and high and deep is the love of Christ." **Ephesians 3:17-18**

Maybe it's because of my calling or perhaps my Mum; I love talking about God. I became a believer as a teen, and before then, although I was oblivion to the depth of God's love for me because of my parents' walk with Christ, my life was filled with the topic of God. Mum sings and talks about Him like He's right in the room. She wakes us every morning at 6 am to read scriptures, sing a hymn, and pray before we head to school. She repeats the same hymn, prayer, and Bible reading routine at 9 pm each night.

Although Dad was a merchant navy and mostly abroad, when he was home, while he was not as grounded as Mum was in her faith, God was also a significant reference for him. I heard about Job's story so much that, as an adult, I wouldn't say I like reading it because I can almost still hear my dad's voice repeating it repeatedly. I would have appreciated a few minutes of extra sleep those mornings and a longer time watching the television those nights, but the pleasure Mum found in walking with Jesus was the greatest legacy she could offer us.

To my mother, God can't be negotiated for momentary comfort, and she knew that while other things would end, the message of the cross remains. The topic of God is inexhaustible, and for us to see redemption through the death of Christ, we must see life through the splendor of God's creation. It starts in awe of His majesty and continues through eternity in awe of His glory. In a world that moves at a pace like ours, we outrun everything and keep improving on every knowledge, but not the topic of God because He is who He is, and whether we agree or not does not change Him. He is immutable to change, let alone by man's dictate.

Take a minute to think about the different ideologies, innovations, ideas, people, chants, and social causes that have come and gone. Even the innovations and ideology that stay, like electricity or the law of gravity, have lost their wonder in our eyes as we become accustomed to them. Now, close your eyes and envision God; the wonder of His glory is as real and overwhelming as the first time we embrace His love.

One of my life's greatest privileges is to be married to a man who matches my love for God. Christ is our guide, judge, and mediator. We started praying to and talking about

God together about twenty-five years ago and are still talking about Him. We approach His omnipresence in our lives, not spiritually sanctimoniously but in a fatherly, friendly, fun, intentionally conscious way. We keep God at the center of all our activities: play, laugh, cry, walk through misunderstandings, choose career paths, wriggle through stress, pain, joy, plan, and raise our children. We both know that we can only grow apart if we neglect the inexhaustible topic of God while building on things about life.

You will always have something to deliberate on if God is the subject. I've heard about Him for almost fifty years (Mum, Dad, darling husband, friends), and my mind has not scratched the surface of the depth of Him; I want more. If you always want something to discuss with your spouse, talk about God. If you want to have what to talk about with your children, talk about God. If you wish to have friends you'll always enjoy being around, find those who love to talk about God.

God loves everyone and calls us to follow Him, but He leaves us with the choice. The idea that God does not exist is not new and doesn't bother Him or change who He is, but to walk with Jesus, you must first believe in God. Jesus said in John 14:1, "Believe in God, believe also in me." It starts with an awe of God, with an embrace of the beauty of the rugged cross.

LORD, I HAVE A QUESTION

"And this is the confidence that we have in him, that, if we ask anything according to his will, he heareth us: And if we know that he hear us, whatsoever we ask, we know that we have the petitions that we desired of him." **1 John 5:14-15**

I didn't start driving early; when I started, I spent days studying the big book to pass the test. I asked my teacher several questions and watched him show me how to signal, turn the wheel, check the mirror, and other necessary skills. I took the time to learn to ensure I'd be ready to keep myself and everyone around safe when I got behind the wheel.

In a self-righteous stance, many Christians debate the need to ask God questions when we get overwhelmed. We mistake 'Asking' for defiance, believing that asking Him is the same as questioning Him. To question someone is to go off an assumption or argue a point to reach a predetermined conclusion. A Lawyer questions an accused person to support a decision he intends to make. However, asking your teacher questions comes from wanting clarification on a subject. Like a loving teacher should, God loves it when we ask.

The conversation between God and Abraham in **Genesis 18** is intriguing. It reveals God's willingness to welcome questions from His children. First, God said in verse 17, *"Shall I hide from Abraham what I am about to do?"* Even though Abraham knew it was a privilege for God to reveal His plan to him, he didn't hesitate to ask questions, and God didn't discourage him from asking. His confusion about the righteous getting in harm's way because of the wicked made him ask questions. He bargained with God.

When I read that story, I could not help wondering what would have happened if Abraham had continued the negotiation with God. What if he had asked God to spare the nation for the sake of two righteous people? What if he'd volunteered as an evangelist to warn them to repent? Abraham ended the negotiation when he got tired; he stopped at ten. At no point during the conversation did God get angry with him, saying, "Okay, that's enough; you can't ask for more." Abraham reached a limit, but God did not.

A million and one confusing things are happening in our lives daily, and instead of asking God why, what, and how, we simply sit him on the defendant's chair, questioning His goodness. In the pretense of humility, the arrogance of the human spirit believes that asking God questions about things we don't understand is wrong. On the contrary, not asking

Him for help when we need to figure things out is pride and always leads to pain. For example, a person who does not know how to swim and jumps in the pool will drown. We must go through a learning period before we can swim laps. To make it through the oceans of life, take God up on His offer and ask Him questions.

THE PREEMINENCE OF CHRIST'S LORDSHIP

"And He is the head of the body, the church, who is the beginning, the firstborn from the dead, that in all things He may have the preeminence."
Colossians 1:18

If I can believe in the law of seed time and harvest time and the law of the breaking of the dawn, then I believe in the preeminence of the lordship of Christ. If I truly trust the emotional bond I share with my husband, mother, and father and the selfless love I pour on my children, then I can, without any doubt, attribute that nature to God in me. He is the Head of all and begins and ends all things.

The royalty of the Lord Jesus binds the fabric through which the world stands and eternity exits. **John 1:3** says, *"All things were made by Him, and without Him was nothing made that was made."* His glory speaks through the ages, and His reign covers the beginning and end of the universe.

To argue that humanity is sustained by self-reliance is devoid of truth, and to believe that Jesus is Lord sets us on the path of eternal life. It dissipates the fear of the unknown and illuminates the dark places of the soul, setting us free from the bondage of sin and guilt. His majesty covers us with God's love and crowns our limited minds with wisdom. Living conscious of the Lordship of Christ opens our eyes to see the evidence of His glory in the little things that make for life: joy, peace, love, pain, and excitement.

God's love forms the foundation for our existence and extends grace to those who ask. As a product of that love established through Jesus's death and resurrection, we can live free of the bondage of sin. His preeminence is rooted in the depth of His love for humanity, and whether or not you agree, He died that we might live.

The certainty of the lordship of Christ runs parallel to the assurance of God's love for us. It is not tied to the fathomability or the narrow stretch of our human minds. In Him, all things exist, and to venture through life without Him leaves us empty and confused. Paul revealed in **Colossians 1:18b**, *"He is the beginning, the firstborn from the dead, that in all things He may have the preeminence."*

"HEARTITUDE" OF WORSHIP

"I will praise thee with my whole heart: before the gods will I sing praise unto thee. I will worship toward thy holy temple and praise thy name for thy lovingkindness and for thy truth: for thou hast magnified thy word above all thy name."
Psalm 138:1-2

Despite David's despair in **Psalm 43**, his response in verse 4 acknowledges his delight and joy in God. He said, *"Then I will go to the altar of God, to God, my joy and my delight. I will praise you with the lyre, O God, my God."* I can relate because I started college in 1994, during one of the most challenging times for my parents. My Dad retired unexpectedly, which overturned the family lifestyle we were used to. Stepping into a vital stage of my life at such an uneasy time placed a lot of pressure on my young heart and made it tough for me. However, I don't know how I would have succeeded in college without worship.

I could not afford a dorm room, so I lived happily with my sweet old god-grandmother. My best possession was the rundown cassette tape player in the room. Although we only enjoyed electricity a few hours daily and sometimes lived without electricity for days, I maximized every second I got to fill my room with worship. I always had the tape on the floor beside my bed where my hand could easily reach it, even at night.

I remember many days I'd sit in the room crying, unsure of how to tackle the demands of the coming weeks, but worship kept me going. It reinforced my belief that Christ is mindful of my weariness and will uphold me. I knew that somehow, God would see me through each day until I reached the end of the road.

I can unequivocally state that worship got me through college and is getting me through life. It's been decades since I lived in that little room with my rundown tape player, but my encounters with God during those difficult days form the core of my reliance on worship. God saw me through the hopelessness of that season of my life and gave me peace in His presence through worship. My encounters with the calming presence of God through prayer make it easier for my heart to respond to the sound of worship regardless of my situation.

Worship is a matter of your heart. It is not just the singing and melody that comes from the sweetest lungs or strings of the grandest harp. It's personal, even in a crowd of a million people. We don't have to sing it for our hearts to respond to it. Worship is the constant posture of acknowledging God's love and sovereignty and remembering that even if things are not working according to our expectations, God is still who He is.

Our circumstances don't have to be perfect for our worship to be perfect. Whether we are at the top of the mountain or walking through a valley doesn't matter. We can be overwhelmed or elated. We can sit, stand, cry at the feet of Christ, or raise our hands to express surrender and gratitude in worship. When we understand the power of God's presence through worship, our heart responds in awe of our maker.

INTENTIONALLY CHRISTIAN

*"Therefore, since we are surrounded by such a great
cloud of witnesses, let us throw off everything that
hinders and the sin that so easily entangles. And let us
run with perseverance the race marked out for
us. Fixing our eyes on Jesus, the pioneer and perfecter
of faith. For the joy set before Him, he endured the
cross, scorning its shame, and sat down at the right
hand of the throne of God."* **Hebrews 12:1-2**

Although I have nothing against New Year's resolutions, I've not subscribed to them since I became a Christian. They place excessive demands on my humanity. In addition, they emphasize things I need to accomplish for myself and less about the God side of the deal: lose weight, get a degree, change my fashion sense, or advance in a career.

Of course, pausing to evaluate the past to assess the future with fewer ambiguities is important; however, I must do so in cognizance of God's purpose for my life. My husband and I always plan for the year and press the reset buttons where necessary, but it's more geared toward growth and God than our personal needs. We might have to change a few things here and there, but they must reflect God in us and our lives together. When Christ is the motivation, God is committed to accomplishing them.

Perhaps you have succeeded in making yearly resolutions and keeping them; I applaud you and encourage you to continue. After all, **1 Timothy 4:8** states, *"Bodily exercise profits, little."* However, as you set your resolutions in motion, remember the concluding part of that same verse, which says, *"But godliness is profitable unto all things, having promise of the life that now is, and of that which is to come."*

Watch your steps as you begin each year because it's so easy to be entangled when caught in a web. To avoid getting caught in one, allow God to light your path. Don't walk around or play with sin because one sin will lead to another, holding you captive. A bug that steps into a spider's web stares in the face of hopelessness, and every move leads to further entanglement. The best defense is to avoid getting caught up in it to avoid being roped.

As I continue this journey with Christ, my heart continues to beat louder in harmony with the sound of Heaven. A sound that calls me beyond the comfort I've created for myself to live for something within a scope I built. The echoes of Heaven usher me on the path that accomplishes God's will for my world, friends, and the people He sends my way. In that, I find rest in my purpose. It's becoming less about Martha and more about "As it is in Heaven."

To be intentionally Christian, we'll approach each day, situation, action, and reaction from Heaven's view lens, conscious of our identity and the kingdom we represent. God calls us to step out of the sidelines, where 'Self' rules, and run the race He sets before us (**Hebrews 12:1-2**). Serve others, encourage the weary, pray for your friends, the church of Christ, and the lost, and ask God to put you to work for kingdom purposes. The baton of righteousness is in our hands, and we must move at a pace that honors the sacrifices of Christ.

WHAT TOMORROW HOLDS

"The Lord himself goes before you and will be with you; he will never leave you nor forsake you. Do not be afraid; do not be discouraged."
Deuteronomy 31:8

Thank God we made it! We've stepped into another season and the beginning of a future we get to create with God. Although the past years had many challenges, He remained God at each turn. Despite the uproar, anxiety, and confusion, we were shielded by His goodness.

God was faithful to His promises to never leave nor forsake us, even in the darkest seasons. He lifted us above the high waters and gave us hope to face another morning. He wiped our tears away when we cried, leading us beside the still waters. Although our legs were unstable along the way, He held us up with His outstretched arms. Like David, although we walked in the valley of the shadow of death, He was with us to light our paths. He paved a road for us in the wilderness and caused the sun to break through our death valleys.

God always comes through for His own and hides them under the shadow of His wings. Just as every valley has surrounding mountains, and every darkest hour has the dawn of the day in its morning, we stand assured that we are not alone. For all He is, I will put my last drop of blood on the line to choose God's faithfulness over the fear of tomorrow. And fight the good fight of faith with Him by me over complacency.

As lifelong benefactors of God's goodness and salvation in Christ, despite all the weight placed on us by the world and our brokenness, I dare say, "GOD IS GOOD!" He is the reason we are still standing and the hope in our hopelessness. We have no idea what tomorrow holds, but one thing is sure: the Almighty God has gone before us, and we are not afraid. Not because we have things figured out but because we walk with the 'I AM.' He is the Father who never fails and always sticks around no matter how messy the journey gets.

CALL HIM, JESUS

*"She will give birth to a son, and you are to give him the name Jesus because he will save his people from their sins." **Matthew 1:21***

Why has the story of the baby born in a manger captivated humanity generation after generation? It's not a typical heroic story saturated with valor and splendor but one simplified by love. Despite the consistent efforts to reduce its validity, the story keeps reaching hearts from one end of the earth to the other. Something about the Christmas story clarifies the confusion about our existence and the possibility of walking with God on this side of eternity.

The birth of Christ marks the beginning of a new era for humanity. It changes everything and beats the devil's imagination to conquer sin, shame, and condemnation. In ignorance, the devil must have thought, "What can a little boy in a manger do to me, and how can He save humanity from their sins? The devil knew the King was here and tried to stop Him but lost at each turn, even when he thought otherwise.

The details of Christ's birth were written to honor the order of life, and God personified His earth's visit through a simple story set in Bethlehem to rescue mankind. It turned the tides in favor of humanity and prepared our route back to our Heavenly Father. The beauty and enduring truth in God's demonstration of love through the birth of Christ is not because of glamor or fame; it's because it's the story of love in a human child.

When the angel appeared to Joseph in **Matthew 1:21** and told him to name the baby Jesus, Joseph honored God and married his betrothed. He loved her and protected his unborn child, not knowing he was part of a story that would grow to be the deepest-rooted tree of love for humanity. He could not have imagined what the name Jesus would mean to the world; he could not fathom beyond where a chariot could reach.

The name of Jesus, spoken in any language, delivers the same power accorded by God thousands of years ago. Its potency to save, forgive, heal, soothe, comfort, and uplift remains the same today, just as it was yesterday and forever will be. The mere mention of Jesus sends a million redeemed souls shouting in joy. Jesus won in birth, death, and resurrection, and He continues to win in all conversations and the lives of all who call Him Lord.

AN ORANGE IN A BOWL OF APPLES

"Finally, brothers and sisters, whatever is true, whatever is noble, whatever is right, whatever is pure, whatever is lovely, whatever is admirable—if anything is excellent or praiseworthy—think about such things."
Philippians 4:8

When Beaver and his friends in the sixty's sitcom "Just Leave It to Beaver" decided to wear their monster sweatshirts to school, he ignored his parents' instruction and wore the shirt anyway. When the school reported him to his parents, he told his dad he wore the shirt because he thought the other boys would do the same. Thinking that he could hide his wrongs in the crowd, he was surprised that his friends decided against the choice to disobey their parents and left him to face the consequences of his actions.

Like Beaver, it's easy to hide behind the crowd, but ultimately, we will face the consequences of every decision. The distinguishing line between right and wrong is shrinking daily because the simple judgment of right or wrong no longer measures our morality scale. We seek the crowd's verdict before we verify if our choices are godly or align with God. We often think if we have others doing it, then it must be acceptable. We take actions before weighing them on the scale of eternity or taking the time to measure the cost for our soul's health.

We are each an entity created with willpower, and we can choose right or wrong. An orange in a bowl of apples doesn't become an apple, and one wrong in a million rights doesn't become right. Wrong will always be wrong, even if it hides in an ocean of rights. It takes you to make that choice because there'll be no one behind 'You' to help justify your decisions here on earth when you stand alone before God.

Paul said in **Philippians 4:8**, '*Think*.' The crowd that voted for Christ to be crucified did not think because if they did, they would remember how He healed the blind, raised the dead, fed the hungry, and touched every life He encountered. He did no wrong, yet they condemned Him. He was the best thing that happened to humanity, and they missed it because they muddled right with wrong.

At the end of the episode, Beaver's Dad explains to him why his choice to disobey his parents was wrong. He said, "It's still wrong, no matter how many people do it. Wrong is wrong even when everyone else says it's right, and right is right even when everyone else says it's wrong." If we look beyond our worldly affiliations to narrow our decision-making to align with the will of God, it won't matter what the crowd thinks; it will only matter if, in God's order of life and godliness, it's right or wrong. You are an entity, and your choices are yours, regardless of the chants you join in.

FAITHFULLY CHRISTIAN

*"Know therefore that the Lord your God is God; he is the faithful God, keeping his covenant of love to a thousand generations of those who love him and keep his commandments." **Deuteronomy 7:9***

I have signed off a few letters and received a few endings with 'Yours Faithfully." We adopted these two words as a sign of formality and a simple way to end a message. However, until a recent study in my Bible group, I never thought much about growing in faithfulness as a fruit of the Spirit. I say and write it, but never beyond formality.

Faithfulness is a fundamental attribute of God. It walks hand in hand with hope and speaks directly of God's nature and His promises to us. God's hope in humanity is tied to His faithfulness. For instance, because of His faithfulness, He was committed to His promise to rescue us from our sins, and despite our disobedience, He still sent Christ to die for us. But for faithfulness, God would have given up on humanity long before Jesus showed up on the scene. Faithfulness is consistent, and one never gives up hope.

I've heard messages and read different books on the Fruits of the Spirit, but the focus usually rests on goodness, kindness, and others, but hardly faithfulness. Perhaps this is because we think it's not a fruit that can be developed in us by the Holy Spirit, or maybe faithfulness is reserved only for God. However, if God does not believe it's a fruit we need, it won't be listed as part of the fruits of the Spirit.

My husband is the most faithful person in my life; he stands as a warrior no matter what life throws at me because our hearts pant toward Jesus. His faithfulness is not momentary or seasonal; it's a nature every godly man shares with God. Also, although I lost my Mum years ago, I've been blessed by a woman who has stood in her place for decades. She loves God, and His nature of faithfulness is evident in all her relationships. Although she didn't get any material reward for her kindness, she would fast and pray if she knew I was going through a difficult season.

Being faithful goes beyond what others can see and reward you for. It cannot be masked by our brokenness or feigned by our human ego. It calls for a significant dedication to drill our core to reveal the heart of God. I knew that when I asked God to teach me how to be a faithful Christian, He would walk me through unfamiliar roads, but I was unprepared for the demands of being faithful. It was easier to practice goodness through hospitality because all I needed to do was send a gift, a kind note, or show up for a few minutes. Faithfulness demands more; it sounds the alarm at odd times of the day and places me in awkward situations that challenge my comfort.

Living as a faithful Christian means you are in partnership with God for a particular person, place, or thing, and you are ready to pray, cry, and tarry as long as it requires until they make it through your challenges. It's the most selfless attribute a Christian can grow in because it pulls from within to reflect without. It doesn't give instant gratification but offers prolonged long-suffering with others. Faithfulness to others makes you stand by them as they endure difficult seasons. It strengthens you to hold their hands, determined not to let go. It would wake you up in the middle of the night to pray for a neighbor, a friend, or a co-worker until God sees them through.

Lamentations 3:22-23-, describes God's faithfulness as something renewed daily. It says, *"Because of the Lord's great love, we are not consumed, for his compassions never fail. They are new every morning; great is your faithfulness."* To cultivate that nature of God, we must live above the confines of "Me, myself, and I" to be available to hold the hands of the weak and pray with the weary because, in our faithfulness, we express God's love.

WORTH MORE THAN MANY SPARROWS

*"And even the very hairs of your head are all numbered. So don't be afraid; you are worth more than many sparrows." **Matthew 10:30-31***

In a world filled with castles of pride, where people always want to find a way to put themselves above others, it's important to know who you are as a child of God. The value man places on you cannot compare to the worth God places on you. David was privy to this mystery and enjoyed a relationship with God in a way that defied man's interference. Even when he missed the mark, he understood the depth of the Father's love, and he knew God would never leave nor forsake him.

I have been guilty of mentally evaluating people's worth, and I have had my share of walking into a room and my worth being evaluated by the people in it because they believed they knew me based on what they could see. Because she's a woman, she's worth this; because of the color of her skin, she's worth that; because she has a particular level of education, she's worth this. However, when you put all the worldly attributes together and place them on a scale, it still can't compare to a drop of the ocean of love the Father places you.

Living to please men instead of God wastes affection because you can never match up to the demands of men, yet you are worth more than a million of it. To wake up in the morning knowing who you are in the eyes of your Father pushes you beyond the limits of satisfaction established by man's broken nature. It reminds you that although you might be going through an alley of uncertainty, you know that God's love will walk you through it.

Regardless of your present situation, where you live or work, what you look like, your country of origin, or the dollar amount in your bank, you are treasured by God. Praying in **Psalm 17:8**, David said, *"Keep me as the apple of your eye; hide me in the shadow of your wings."* He knew he was the apple of God's eye and prayed that God should keep him there. Knowing you are the apple of God's eyes puts your value in a clearer perspective.

Stop moving to the drumbeats of man's illusion of who you are; they don't know you. You are worth more than any mind can fathom. Start dancing to the songs of Heaven because your Father's heartbeat is filled with love for you. God is mindful of you. Every tear, every smile, and every moment of your life count in Heaven's calendar because you are worth more than many sparrows.

I WILL SAY TO MY SOUL

*"Because of the Lord's great love, we are not consumed, for his compassions never fail. They are new every morning; great is your faithfulness… The Lord is good to those whose hope is in him, to the one who seeks him." **Lamentations 3:22-23,25***

Talking from a place of God's goodness comes from the seed of gratitude and intentionality. It's not the human default because we are wired to think of what doesn't work and ignore what does. While God permits challenges and lavishes us with love in our seasons of pain, it's always good to speak from a place of His goodness despite our circumstances. We can't reduce God to a moment in time because of weariness when He wraps the universe, defining times and seasons in His hands.

It takes reminding our soul as Luke said in **Luke 12:19**, *"And I will say to my soul, Soul, thou hast many goods laid up for many years; take thine ease, eat, drink, and be merry."* While there are a million and one reasons why we

178

should focus on the obstacles and cliffs we scale over daily, the goodness of God speaks louder. It speaks to the deepest part of our souls because the longer we walk with God, the more our soul responds to the truth of His goodness.

The Book of Lamentations is filled with emotions but still speaks of God's goodness. In chapter 3, verse 25, it says, *"The Lord is good,"* meaning that for every single reason to bury yourself in gloom, there are a million reasons to remember God's goodness. If all you can do at the moment of your trials is focus on the undeniable truth of God's presence, it will revitalize you for the journey ahead.

When we glorify our emotions above God, they consume us. Yes, I also experience the dark side of life, and yes, my spirit gets rattled. However, I want to speak from a place of His goodness and not my weakness. I want to talk of the little lamp He shines on my path to break through the thick darkness more than the darkness itself. I want my focus to be on the safe boat He provides to carry me through the roaring sea more than the vastness of the sea. I want to speak from a place of all the triumphs I've enjoyed walking with God more than the battles I've faced.

When I do that, I remind my soul and the people around me that I live conscious of the God I'm walking with, not what Martha can and cannot do. I see beyond the waves because if I keep my eyes on the sea, it will drown me. Additionally, if I focus on the darkness long enough, it will blind me. The ultimate truth is I'm not walking alone, and the one who stands by me is worthy of all adoration.

PART VI

THE IMMACULATE GLORY OF TODAY

"This is the day the Lord has made; We will rejoice and be glad in it." **Psalm 118:24**

We often place a massive demand on our history to determine our present and future realities and, in turn, reduce the immaculate glory of today. While our past plays a significant role and is relevant for our present, and our present is vital for our future, it's crucial to learn how to build from it to avoid the pitfalls of the past. Although life might not always go as planned, things left to chance have a greater risk of failure.

Like any human, I've made many mistakes and continue to, but they don't define me; God does. Don't give in to the voices of failure ringing in your ears; if you have today, tomorrow can be better. Just because you are swamped with lies does not mean you will fail. Remember that the story of one is not the story of all. Yesterday has passed, and we must give today a fighting chance to experience a better tomorrow by aligning our feet with God's footsteps.

Yes, despite the failed marriages all around you, yours can be exceptional, and despite the many vices experienced by the younger generation, your children can be taught of God. If you throw in the towel, telling yourself, "What's the point?" you will deny tomorrow the fruits from the seed that needs to be planted today.

I approach everything I hope for with a sense of intentionality, minding the daily demands more than the echoes of yesterday. My parents' marriage might not have been the best in the world, but I'm building on the beauty and the misses, and I hope my children build better marriages from learning from mine. To experience what I want in my marriage, I must invest daily. Also, to achieve the closeness I hope for between my children and their walk with God, I must be mindful of creating an environment for them to develop and nurture growth daily.

I've realized that while God's intent is for me to have a great future rooted in hope (**Jeremiah 29:11**), there is no wand waving by my creator to make my dreams come true. By His design, we all have a part to play in achieving our desires in life. Although perfection is an unending process, God has woven the ability to make things better within each redeemed soul and the possibility to make today better than yesterday. So, learn to sit at the feet of Christ to make today glorious because while you can't do anything to remedy yesterday, today is another opportunity to create a better tomorrow.

GOD, DON'T WORRY, I GOT THIS!

"Search me, God, and know my heart; test me and know my anxious thoughts. See if there is any offensive way in me and lead me in the way everlasting." **Psalm 139:23-24**

A man's character is tested when he feels he's at the top of his game. It's easier to acknowledge God when we are at our breaking point, but when the road seems smooth enough, we tend to take the steering wheel from Him, saying, "God, don't worry, I got this." Our actions toward God and people must be guided by scriptural principles that act as barriers against pride and prejudice.

When we don't measure our hearts on the scale of godly preference, we open the doors to abusing our freedom as heirs of the kingdom of God and bearers of the mark of Christ. There is a direct correlation between culture and honoring God with how we live and treat others. Ignoring the little nudge in our hearts that pushes us to act differently or respond differently will lead us to a downward spiral if we don't heed Heaven's caution signs.

We have nothing to lose walking with God, but we must do so and be ready to grow and learn as He leads us. You can hand your life over to Christ and yet dictate how you want to live it, or you can hand it to Him and allow Him to guide you. It's a conscious and continuous choice we have to make. Because if a man chooses to be the ruler and lord over his castle, his heart is in danger of sliding down a murky path of "Pridetitude" (Pride attitude).

Like the saying, "You can't eat your cake and have it," you can't guide yourself through life independent of godly principles and expect godly results. To trust God to lead, He has to be the leader, not the student. We can't stand behind Him, telling Him where to turn and how to navigate like He is a student in our driving school. Until we live intentionally caring about the health of our hearts, the bumps on the road will trip us to a hard fall.

TWO SIDES TO THE COIN-
GOD OR NOT GOD

*"Then Moses stood in the gate of the camp and said, who is on the Lord's side? Let him come unto me. And all the sons of Levi gathered themselves together unto him." **Exodus 32:22***

When Moses went up to the mountain to meet with God, it left the children of Israel vulnerable to going back to their old ways. They demanded that Aaron make them a graven image to worship instead of the God who delivered them from captivity. Despite the exploits they saw God did, the plagues in Egypt, parting the sea, and feeding them in the wilderness, they forgot that though they've not seen Him, He is sovereign in their affairs. Their faith wavered because it was not rooted deep enough for them to triumph without a godly leader.

Many Christians sit on the fence, navigating between their belief in Christ's love for them and their desire to hold on to other things that do not glorify God. They hop between the church and ungodly places, ignoring the nudging of the Holy Spirit. Because they've not devoted time to learning at Jesus's feet, their understanding of God's majesty is shuffled with worldly desires.

I hear references to grey areas, but they don't apply to life and godliness. There are simply two sides to the coin: good or evil, life or death, Heaven or hell, and it takes walking with God always (Not based on intellect or culture) to choose right. One side cost Jesus the cross, and the other will cost us eternity. We are all limited to trusting God or satisfying our desires. We either walk with God or walk alone. Even in death, there's no hovering around the galaxies or swimming in oblivion because our choice now will determine our eternal destiny.

When Moses told the children of Israel to decide, they had just two choices. They could separate themselves from their man-made graven image to cross to the Lord's side or stay on the opposite side of the mountain. There were no in-between options. God's offer of redemption is free, but there's no in-between choice for us to sit and swing our legs on the fence. When we accept Christ, we are either all in with Christ or not in at all. Choosing whose side you're on is not a daily flip of the coin. Following Christ means you must live for God, and your life should always reflect your choice.

I KNOW A SECRET PLACE

"He that dwelleth in the secret place of the Most High shall abide under the shadow of the Almighty. I will say of the Lord; He is my refuge and my fortress: my God; in him will I trust." **Psalm 91:1-2**

Psalm 91 is one of my favorite scriptures. Growing up, I had to read it multiple times, sometimes daily, because it was also one of my Mum's go-to Psalms. It's a Psalm that reveals the confidence of walking with God. It does not deny the presence of evil; it simply affirms God's power and faithfulness. It talks about the man who dwells in the secret place of the Most High and his adventure with God.

He is fully aware of God's presence. He knows that just because he lives under the protection of the Most High does not exclude him from walking through the snare of the fowler and noisome pestilence. He fights with a thousand on one side and another thousand on the other. He faces the lion, the adder, and the dragon and overcomes them because God is with him.

I know a hand that can hold you, a voice that can soothe you, and a place that can hide you. I've enjoyed the whispers of Heaven, the cuddles of my Father's arm, and the shade of His wings enough to know He is faithful. There's no roar loud enough to drown God or river too deep to overwhelm His presence. No matter where life leads, I know He never leaves nor forsakes His own. You can come with all the baggage that weighs you down and lay it right at the foot of the cross, leaning on Him.

I've walked a few miles of discomfort several times, and the only constant factor through each battle is the presence of God. Dwelling in His secret place gives you a million edge over the enemy: you become untouchable. It means your adventure through life will not be alone; the Almighty will be with you, give His angels charge over you, and deliver you. The destiny of the man or woman who dwells under the shadow of the God of Zion is sealed in victory.

WHEN GOD'S GIRLS MEET

"There is a river whose streams make glad the city of God, the holy place where the Most High dwells. God is within her; she will not fall; God will help her at break of day." **Psalm 46"4-5**

I was so excited when I received a text from a friend I'd not seen in about four years, asking to meet for lunch because she was in town. I replied to Patty's text that night, telling her I'd be there. I also texted her before leaving home the next day to let her know I was on my way and would see her in about thirty minutes.

Unknown to me, she did not see my texts and decided her husband would drop her off at the public library. When I got to the address she sent, she was surprised to receive my call because she thought I hadn't responded to her text and wouldn't show up. Regardless, I was determined to see her, so we drove to the library, where I saw her sitting on the bench outside.

After the hugs, we were about to walk inside to find a place to sit and talk when we saw Anna, a mutual friend, entering the library. Two weeks before that day, I spent time with Anna, sharing our hearts for Christ, the Kingdom, and the depth to which we believe God is calling us. However, although the three of us were in the Women's SOAP ministry together years prior, we have not been in the same space since 2019 because Patty relocated.

Anna told us about the unusual circumstances that led her to the library; like us, she wasn't supposed to be there but came anyway. At that point, we all knew there was more to our meeting; we realized God was knitting the stories together for us to meet there. God divinely crafted it, and we treated that time with awe of our Heavenly Father.

A few weeks prior, I told my husband I felt a need that many women are seeking to dig deeper in their walk with Jesus. I told him I didn't know how, but I believed God was making room for Christian women to ascend to higher realms in their walk with Him. I felt a call to go beyond being rattled by our emotions and geared by the affirming call of God over each of our lives.

I love God-ordained moments, and I don't take them for granted. That might not be the first time Patty would be visiting, but God had plans for that day. The dots between the lines and the complexity of how they met in that space and time can't be coincidental in the best man-written story. We were not supposed to be there but somehow ended up there.

While there were people around us that afternoon, they did not deter us from drawing from the river of grace inside one another. In the library's restaurant, we talked about God and His purpose for our lives, the church, and the world. We sat at the library's restaurant for two hours, and it felt like minutes. I was so fired up that I wrote a months-worth article for 'Abiding Christian' the next day.

Sitting between these two women in the most unlikely place that day was somewhat overwhelming, and it triggered a resolve to ignite that same awesome feeling in my Christian friends. We are more than pretty faces in pretty dresses; we are warriors of an eternal Kingdom. I know it doesn't matter where, how, when, or what age we are. It only matters who we are: daughters of Zion.

I believe God is calling an assemble, telling us to push beyond our comfort zone, heed the clarion sound, and walk in His call over our lives. The world might underestimate the power of "The one" that chases a thousand, but "The two" that chases ten thousand (**Deuteronomy 32:20**) is a different story. We are here for a reason, in the time and space that God places us in, and maximizing His grace to show forth His glory always puts us ahead of the devil's wiles.

THE HANDS MOLDING ME

"He said, "Can I not do with you, Israel, as this potter does?" declares the Lord. "Like clay in the hand of the potter, so are you in my hand, Israel."
Jeremiah 18:6

It's incredible what can come out of an unassuming, shapeless clay. One day, it's all dirt, cracked, and formless; the next, it's a priced centerpiece on a dining table because the potter looked at it and said, "I can do something with that." For a bowl of clay to become a treasured jar, it must submit itself to the hands of the potter. It must trust the process it has to go through in the potter's house. It will be punched, watered, bent, trimmed, molded, and passed through fire.

The house of the potter, who created the grandest works of art, might not be the cleanest to walk into because of all the unfinished molds on his table, floor, and against his walls. He might have streaks of clay in the wrong places and broken vessels lying all around, but he is nonetheless a creator of amazing artworks. Therefore, it is safe to assume that a potter is devoted to making his masterpiece as envisioned if the clay continues to be subject to the making process. I live in the Potter's house, so I should know.

The triviality of the human heart baffles me. Our brokenness limits us, yet we elevate our souls above the one God who holds it all: the power to make us perfect. We've captured and embraced characteristics and values that need to submit themselves in the hands of our maker. As clay in the potter's house, we are a continuous work in progress, and there's always a hole to block, a bulge to smooth out, and room for growth.

Isaiah said, *"Yet you, Lord, are our Father. We are the clay; you are the potter; we are all the work of your hand,"* **Isaiah 64:8**. It takes clay that knows its place to become what the potter wants it to be. A clay that assumes the potter's role would not just remain ordinary; it would become drier and worse than its original state.

I am a willing lump of clay in the potter's house. I already know there is no completion on this side of Heaven, so before you count me out or define me as useless, look beyond my lumps and holes and see the hands molding me. Like a dry, unassuming clay in the potter's house, I was defined as "Perfect" the day I chose to live at the foot of the cross and submit my life to the supremacy of Christ. I'm a shapeless clay in the potter's hands. You might not see it yet, but God is making something extraordinary from my imperfections.

EVERYTHING BUT CHRIST

"And this I do for the gospel's sake, that I might be partaker thereof with you." **1 Corinthians 19:21**

Before Saul's encounter with Christ, one can say he had it all: fame, wealth, affluence, and education. He was a cultural star of his time. He had it all through a layman's eyes because the missing cord to the fullness of life lies in the secret place of the depth of every man's soul.

In chapter 3, verses 4 through 7, writing to the Philippians, Paul cites himself as having good reasons to glory in his earthly exploits. He said that despite all he was before Christ, a circumcised Pharisee and of the revered tribe of Benjamin, nothing compares to following Jesus. To him, trading his walk with Christ for anything was never an option. He wrote in verse 7, *"But whatever were gains to me I now consider loss for the sake of Christ."*

It's believed that life is worth what you put into it, but the truth is, every treasure we stack up will lose its worth if

Christ is not the foundation. A man or woman can choose adultery or material gains over the sanctity of their marriage because of the missing cord of surrender. And these desires may consume them until they align themselves with God. Choosing Christ is a response to the choice He already made at Calvary, which is to die for our sake. He gave it all up in those gruesome hours to offer us a way out of our helplessness.

Everything that brings me joy in life does so because of Christ. My husband, children, Church, and friends are all part of the puzzle, and if you remove Christ from the foundation, it will all crumble. In the same vein, every worry, gloomy night, and uncertainty of life rests on my foundation in Christ, which makes it easy to press forward daily.

Putting my life on a scale that leaves God out of the equation makes it lighter than a feather, weightless, worthless. He is the only anchor that can hold you grounded and the foundation on which any life can have true meaning. There is a resolve to follow Christ that makes Him enough. It leads on a path of peace and satisfaction that makes you know that if you must choose, you'll let go of everything but Christ.

AUTHENTICALLY CHRISTIAN

*"What a wretched man I am! Who will rescue me
from this body that is subject to death? Thanks be to
God, who delivers me through Jesus Christ our Lord!
So then, I myself, in my mind, am a slave to God's
law, but in my sinful nature, a slave to the law of sin."*
Romans 7:24-25

If we think of the Apostle Paul, our minds go to his direct encounter with Jesus and the years he spent planting Churches and ministering the gospel. He is our big brother and one worthy of emulation in every way. However, his humanity is evident in his letter to the Romans. In chapter 7, without referencing a particular sin, he explained his struggles navigating his walk with God and being subject to his sinful nature. He said in verse 18, *"For I do not do the good I want to do, but the evil I do not want to do—this I keep on doing."*

The belief that salvation terminates our default to be defiant to God leads us down the path that separates us farther from the grace that exists through the continuous stream of atonement at Calvary. Being born again does not put us above the law; rather, it awakens the nature of God in us. This nature convinces us to acknowledge and resist sin. We know what sin is because we know what righteousness is, and if you call the sinners' circle, Christians should be the first to fill the lot. More than anyone else, we know that without Christ, we are unworthy to be called saints.

As Christians, we walk in freedom rooted in grace. While sin will always knock on our doors daily, we have the power through Christ to stand firm in righteousness. This does not mean we affirm our mistakes or pat ourselves on the back when we fall. Although we live as overcomers in brokenness, we call sin by its name and subject it to the foot of the cross. We say no to it when it raises its ugly head because the nature of God within us convicts us.

To be authentically Christian means I am a human who, by grace, lives above the faulty, broken, confused, sinful, prideful, and selfish nature I was born with. Although I live in the flesh, I do not walk by the flesh. I may fall a million times, but I will always rise and keep moving toward the mark of the high calling in Christ Jesus. To be authentically Christian does not erase my humanity; it simply means I am enveloped in the purity and perfection of my Savior.

AS IT PERTAINS TO LIFE AND GODLINESS

*"His divine power has given us everything we need for a godly life through our knowledge of him who called us by his own glory and goodness." **2 Peter 1-3***

O ur adoption into the family of God comes with a visa to journey to Heaven with the help of the Holy Spirit. Peter was speaking specifically to the church in **2 Peter 1**. He spoke about walking in God's divine nature and continuing his call for godly living; he said in **2 Peter 1:4**, *"Through these, he has given us his very great and precious promises, so that through them you may participate in the divine nature, having escaped the corruption in the world caused by evil desires."*

To walk the imaginary thin line between enjoying life and pleasing Christ, we fall prey to the perils of our desires, allowing them to hold us captive to emotions already conquered at the cross. There are no lines between pleasing God and enjoying the fullness of life; the fullness of life comes from walking with Jesus and evaluating our lives' worth on the scale of godliness. And it is only by walking with Him that our synergy sings in perfect harmony.

Until we begin to put every aspect of our lives in light of godliness, they will always misalign on the balancing scale of their worth. God is a perfector and loves to see His children thrive; however, we must be subject to His will and live free from disobedience. When we look at the world around us through the lens of godliness, we approach the brokenness plaguing it with empathy instead of condemnation and hands clamped in prayer instead of fists ready to fight.

Living in godliness means placing God at the center of every decision, thought, action, or reaction. It means the job you wake up early to do every day will become more about contributing to your world and not just an avenue to make a living or endure. It means raising your children will be regarded as a ministry and less burdensome. It means you will see your spouse through the eyes of the Father and treat them more intentionally as equal heirs of Christ.

While no formulas excuse us from experiencing difficult seasons, living life through the lens of godliness puts things in a clearer perspective. It helps us define the challenging seasons as training grounds and breakthroughs and triumph seasons as praising grounds. It leads us to enjoy all God purposed for us and ride through bumping roads in anticipation of a better tomorrow.

THE DOOR AT THE WIT' S END

"Then Joseph said to his brothers, "Come close to me." When they had done so, he said, "I am your brother Joseph, the one you sold into Egypt! And now, do not be distressed and do not be angry with yourselves for selling me here because it was to save lives that God sent me ahead of you." **Genesis 45:4-5**

The story of Joseph is one of the greatest comeback stories of all time. It is filled with love, hate, betrayal, abandonment, favor, and forgiveness. He started as the favorite of his father and the most hated by his brothers. He was sold into slavery and landed in the home of a master who loved him and a mistress who desired him. If not for God at the core of his life, Joseph's lineage would have ended with him dead at the hands of his brothers or in prison for a crime he didn't commit.

No matter who we are, we will all eventually reach our wits' ends. However, where the door at the end of those wits ends leads depends on the train we are riding on. If we've made ourselves the author and finisher of our own story, it might lead us to a state of hopelessness, but if we've trusted Christ with our world, it will surely lead to rest.

I've walked through the doors at my wit's end multiple times, and each time has led me on a path paved with grace and patience with God. Like David, while I do not have control over the challenges the world throws at me, I have control over who I trust with them. And whether in rain or sun, it's impossible for Him to fail. **Psalm 121:5-6** says, *"The Lord watches over you, the Lord is your shade at your right hand; the sun will not harm you by day, nor the moon by night."*

To say that Joseph knows what pain is—is putting things mildly because each time he believes he has reached a resting season, he is sent through a different maze. Like I've done severally, I can imagine him sitting in a corner, asking why. "I love my brothers dearly; why do they hate me?" "I serve my master faithfully; why should the wife seduce me?" Other people's actions were beyond his control, but they placed him at the story's center anyway.

As long as we keep Christ as the laser through which the maps of our lives are drawn, He will always catch us before we hit the ground. If you are a child of God, the door at your wit's end won't thrust you down from a mountain peak; it will rest you in the hands of God. Even when everything around you seems to be spinning in a sphere, the loving gaze of Christ will keep you steady.

THAT I MAY GAIN CHRIST

"But whatever were gains to me, I now consider loss for the sake of Christ. What is more, I consider everything a loss because of the surpassing worth of knowing Christ Jesus my Lord, for whose sake I have lost all things. I consider them garbage, that I may gain Christ." **Philippians 1:7-8**

I've been in this world for some decades, and I've seen wealth, health, fame, and glory fade with time. It seems like the more people have, the less worth they feel, leading them to seek more. And no matter what height we attain, it always comes down to the fact that only God can fill the missing piece at our core.

What is that thing that is worth more than what Christ provides for us? If we live in a house that spans miles long and own all the wealth in the world, will it soothe our souls' longing for rest in its maker? If we hold a galaxy each to ourselves, will it reduce our need for a Savior?

Humanity's shortcomings lie in our inability to acknowledge God's sovereignty and surrender in total abandonment. For Christ's sake, it's easy to lay it all down and follow His leadings because He is steadfast in love and grace. What He gives, no one can give or take away.

To gain Christ, we must seek God's heart and will in all our life pursuits because the value of life lies in Christ's accomplished work at Calvary. And we hope to spend eternity with Him. Our wealth is in knowing that we are on the Lord's side and that our heart, although imperfect in this mortal state, is panting after its maker with every beat.

I lay it all down: my hope, fear, strength, and weakness, that I may gain Christ. Paul said in **Philippians 1:7**, *"I consider everything a loss because of the surpassing worth of knowing Christ."* Knowing Jesus tops all valor and conquests. He is my abundance, my sufficiency, my all, and nothing can take the place of His Majesty in this world or in the world to come. The longer I walk with Him and rest on His shoulder, the more I want to be with Him.

BROKEN BUT NOT CONDEMNED

*"He will not break a broken branch or put out a little fire. He will be faithful in making everything fair. He will not lose hope or be crushed until He has made things right on the earth." **Isaiah 42:3-4***

My husband and I were visiting our friends a while ago and saw a pot of planted tomatoes in their garden. The soil looked rich around the plant, and you could see some green tomatoes on the branches of the bent stem. The duct tape around the hanging little plant caught my attention, and we asked why it was wrapped in duct tape. Kasey said that while trying to relocate the plant, the branch broke, and hearing that also broke my heart because I could see how gorgeous the plant was but for the brokenness.

Something resonated in me through this experience. It made me think of myself and others planted in the rich soil of our salvation in the Lord Jesus Christ. Like the broken tomato branch, while still rooted in Him, sometimes circumstances around us move us to breaking point, and instead of standing straight and looking up to Jesus, we are bent over by our brokenness.

I could feel the hurt as my friend explained that the duct tape around the stem was her attempt to save the broken branch and nurse the plant back to life. There was something about the plant that was worth saving, and she was willing to try. This represents the nature of God in our lives because he doesn't let go, even in our brokenness.

Speaking of Jesus, He said in **John 15:1-2**, "*I am the true vine, and my Father is the gardener. He cuts off every branch in me that bears no fruit, while every branch that does bear fruit, he prunes. so that it will be even more fruitful.*" It would have been easier to dispose of the plant if it was unhealthy, with dry-withered stems, leaves, and no fruits. But this was not a lifeless plant; you could see the lush green leaves and the little unripe tomatoes on the branches. It was broken but still rooted, allowing it to flourish again.

The notion that our brokenness is too much for God to handle goes against His nature. As Isaiah said in **Isaiah 42:3**, "*He will not break a broken branch.*" Don't give up because you are broken; God will never give up on you. Our brokenness is just a response to the weight of the wind blowing around us and our mortal limitations. As long as we are rooted in Jesus, we will rise again. Just stay rooted!

About a month after our visit, you can only imagine how excited I was to receive a picture of the plant from Kasey with ripe tomatoes on the wobble branches. The duct tape and the new wire strings around the plant helped nurture it and preserve the fruits. They lived! While God does not need to wrap us in duct tape, He is our source, and sometimes, we need to curdle under His warm embrace and allow Him to nurse us back to life.

YOU ARE CALLED; WALK IN IT

"To some people, the Spirit gives a message of wisdom. To others, the same Spirit gives a message of knowledge. To others, the same Spirit gives faith. To others, that one Spirit gives gifts of healing. To others, he gives the power to do miracles. To others, he gives the ability to prophesy. To others, he gives the ability to tell the spirits apart. To others, he gives them the ability to speak in different kinds of languages they had not known before. And to still others, he gives the ability to explain what was said in those languages." **1 Corinthians 12:8-10**

There's a misconception about the calling of God on His children that has denied the church and the world the magnificence of the united power of the gifts of the Spirit. The brokenness of our humanity has unduly sectioned God's gifts into hierarchies; because you have the gift of leadership, you get to represent Christianity, while others just need to come to Church.

As Christians, it's easy to fall into a routine in our walk with God. We go to church, read the Bible, pray for our daily bread, and repeat. However, while these are fundamental tenets of our faith, there is more to our salvation than these religious routines. Our Christian faith is an adventure. It's a journey that sets us on a course that partners with Christ to extend Calvary to the world around us.

What would the church look like if every Christian operated in their calling? Imagine what the church would look like if those with each gift revealed by Apostle Paul in **1 Corinthians 12** operated in their calling, not for themselves or as a disruption but for the glory of the Father. The church would be filled with prayer warriors and believers who are always ready to serve.

Gifts are lying dormant in the church of Christ. We file in and out every Sunday morning and live below the duplicative power of our redemption. If we can spend decades growing in our careers and societal demands, growing in our understanding of the role God intends for us to play on the grand scale of humanity would change our daily approach to life. Instead of writing 'Me' as the story's hero, it would be more about Christ showing up to touch someone in my life through me.

We are saved to save others, rescued to rescue others, encouraged to encourage others, and healed to heal others. Stepping out of the shadow that clouds God's calling over our lives will mend the broken places we are called to restore and make Heaven closer to our derailing world.

In verse 7 of **1 Corinthians 12**, Paul writes, *"The Holy Spirit is given to each of us in a special way. That is for the good of all."* Stop hiding your gift(s) behind the confines of your walled silos; learn your gifts, and boldly share the bounty of your salvation with the world around you. God assigns a soldier to fix every loophole in the world. If we all live worthy of the call of God over our lives, the world would be better for it.

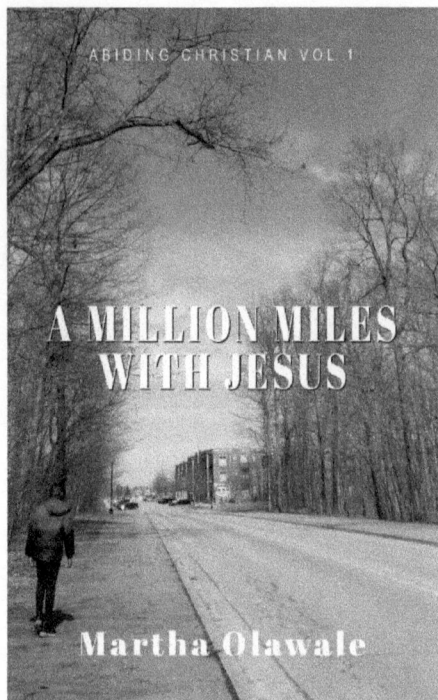

Becoming a Christian starts with a single step, accompanied by a 180-degree turn from where we were to head to where God leads. However, while our repentance leads us in the right direction, we embark on the journey with truckloads of baggage from our past lives, and only Christ can help us walk with the weight off our shoulders. In "A Million Miles with Jesus," the first volume of the Abiding Christian books, you will learn how a first step with Jesus will encourage a million more despite the many oppositions you face.

www.ingramcontent.com/pod-product-compliance
Lightning Source LLC
LaVergne TN
LVHW091251080426
835510LV00007B/214